Exercise
FOR
EVERYONE

Exercise
FOR
EVERYONE

CELEBRITY TRAINER CORNEL CHIN'S
TRIPLE A FITNESS PROGRAMMES FOR
■ ANYONE ■ ANYWHERE ■ ANYTIME

Photography by Graham Atkins Hughes

EDITORIAL DIRECTOR Jane O'Shea
ART DIRECTOR Helen Lewis
DESIGNER Amanda Lerwill
PROJECT EDITOR Hilary Mandleberg
PRODUCTION Jane Rogers

PHOTOGRAPHY Graham Atkins Hughes

First published in 2004 by
Quadrille Publishing Limited
Alhambra House
27–31 Charing Cross Road
London WC2H 0LS

British Library Cataloguing-in-Publication Data. A catalogue
record for this book is available from the British Library.

ISBN 1-84400-086-9

Printed and bound in China

Always consult your doctor before starting a fitness and nutrition
programme if you have any health concerns. This is especially
advised if you are over the age of 40, smoke, are overweight,
have a history of heart disease or are taking any medication.

Contents

Introduction

Welcome to Exercise for Everyone and my Triple A – Anyone, Anywhere, Anytime – exercise plan for life that will guide you to a trimmer, sleeker and more toned you. With Triple A, you can achieve the body you want in the medium term and keep it for the long term, and you don't need any equipment other than an exercise mat or folded towels, a chair or bench and, just occasionally, a pair of dumbbells.

The Triple A system is one that I've developed during my ten years as an independent personal trainer. I use it when training my clients at each and every workout, whether that client is an eminent lawyer, the chairman of a national bank, a film star getting in shape for a particular role, or just an ordinary person.

The idea for Triple A was born when several of my clients came to me for advice on how to maintain their condition while on holiday or on a business trip (some even asked me to go with them!). After all, they didn't want a decline in their level of fitness or to lose the muscle tone they'd worked so hard for. They wanted exercises to do while away from home that would be effective, safe, simple, interesting and not require any equipment. They needed an exercise plan that would enable them to exercise in their hotel room, on the beach or outside in the fresh air. And they also wanted exercises that would not take up too much of their precious time.

No more excuses

How easy is it to make an excuse for not going to the gym or out for a brisk walk or jog around the block? Unless you are a dedicated exercise fanatic, I bet you've thought of all the excuses. Just picture this familiar scenario. You join a swish fitness centre five minutes away by car. Brimming with enthusiasm, you go regularly for the first month, but then your enthusiasm starts to wane. Exercise wasn't as easy as you thought and that five-minute drive to the gym seems like an eternity. Or you arrive home after a hard day's work thinking you'll relax a little before popping out to the gym. Then you look out of the window and it's cold and damp and of course, you don't fancy it. But what if there was an alternative?

Triple A *is* the alternative. It's unique and positive, and because you don't need to go to a gym, it's achievable and realistic. Using the simple principle that 'every bit counts', Triple A makes exercise easier to schedule into hectic days – even if you only have 5 or 10 minutes to spare. Armed with this book, you can be anywhere and working out – even while waiting for the kettle to boil.

Triple A for all

Triple A is for all age ranges and fitness abilities, whether you are a Newcomer, a Restarter, a Regular or a Vigorous exerciser. Each of these four fitness types has its own workout plan, and each is in two parts – an aerobic programme and a toning programme

– uniquely presented so you can see at a glance what you are supposed to be doing. And if you haven't got time to do both parts of the programme, then at least try to do one.

And because, whatever your fitness level, everyone occasionally runs completely out of time, I offer quick-fix programmes for every level – suggestions for a selected handful of exercises that even the most time-challenged person should be able to find time for.

The Newcomer programme is for you if you have very little or no previous experience of exercise. It constitutes the perfect, safe introduction to exercise and its simple, carefully tailored circuit has been devised to help you get started. You should have no trouble with any of the exercises and should find that they are easy to follow and perform – even in the comfort of your own living room.

The Restarter programme is directed at you if you feel you need a 're-introduction' to exercise. Perhaps exercise has been put at the bottom of the list in your ever-changing life priorities. If so, this is the programme that will kick-start the exerciser in you. Take it with you to your hotel room.

The Regular programme is the one to choose if you already engage in some form of exercise or regular sport, perhaps two or three times a week. But what happens to your workouts when you don't have access to the gym or to any equipment? Don't despair. This 'very little equipment required' programme will give you a challenging workout you never thought possible outside of a gym – even in your back garden.

And if you hate the idea of missing any of your frequent exercise sessions, then the Vigorous programme is designed with you in mind. It offers high-intensity training that will leave you dripping in sweat. And the beauty of it is – you don't need any equipment, even on a beach.

Not just exercise

One of my beliefs is that, in order to get the best out of exercise, you need to know a bit about your body and how it functions. That is why, in the first chapter of this book, I address the issues of what makes for fitness and how you can eat to get and stay fit. Many of my clients are concerned about nutrition, especially when they are away from home and their eating can really go haywire – we all know how appetising good hotel or holiday food can be. So I put together a simple eating plan that wouldn't be too restrictive but would also give them choices. The results spoke for themselves as none of them returned from their trips fatter or out of condition. The same could be true for you. I guarantee you'll be thrilled with the results.

The second chapter helps you determine if you are the weight you should be and guides you through some simple fitness tests to show you which of the four exercise programmes is most appropriate for your level of fitness and the goals you are trying to achieve.

In the last chapter I offer my tried-and-tested tips on staying motivated (yes, we all need help sometimes!). And finally, because everyone has questions about fitness, I give you my answers to some of the many I get asked and I take the opportunity to de-bunk a number of the myths surrounding the subject, too. I hope you'll feel better informed once you've read what I have to say.

Now you're about to discover that exercise can be one of life's joys. It energises and gives a sense of wellbeing and accomplishment as well as keeping you fit and healthy. It's never too late to start and by buying this book, you've taken the first step in the right direction. The Triple A exercise programmes presented here are the closest I can get to being your very own personal trainer. So let's get on and further the quest to the new you!

THE
basics
OF FITNESS

This chapter explains some of the basics of how your body works so that once you're seeing the improvements that I promise will happen, you'll have an idea of how they came about. Spend some time reading it before you start to exercise. After all, you wouldn't invest in a company's shares without first studying their accounts, would you? Some of what's here is basic school biology and some is facts about the body that have come to light as a result of recent research. Understanding how we function, the damage we can do to ourselves, whether we really are what we eat and the difference between aerobic and other exercise are all addressed here.

The benefits of exercise

Add life to your years, as well as years to your life, through exercise. We all know that exercise is good for us, but do we actually know why? These are the ten reasons why the medical profession and exercise physiologists tell us we should all embark on some form of regular exercise. I hope these tips will convince you and motivate you further on your pathway to a healthier lifestyle.

Ten reasons why exercise is good for you

1 ENHANCES SELF-IMAGE
Individuals who exercise regularly feel better and more confident about themselves than people who never exercise.

2 REDUCES THE RISK OF HEART DISEASE
Non-exercisers have twice the risk of developing heart disease than those people who exercise on a regular basis.

3 RELIEVES STRESS AND ANXIETY
Exercise dissipates the hormones and other chemicals that build up during periods of great stress. Exercise also generates a period of substantial emotional and physical relaxation that sets in approximately an hour and a half after you've had an intense workout.

4 INCREASES THE GOOD CHOLESTEROL (HDL)
Exercise is one the few things you can do that actually raises the level of good cholesterol (high-density lipoprotein, or HDL) in your bloodstream. HDL is known to lower your risk of heart disease.

5 RELIEVES DEPRESSION
A famous doctor once wrote 'exercise is nature's best tranquilliser'. Mildly to moderately depressed individuals who exercise for 20–30 minutes, three times a week, experience a positive mood swing after only a few weeks.

6 IMPROVES THE QUALITY OF LIFE
Regular exercise will give you more energy to do the activities you enjoy.

7 REDUCES RISK OF CERTAIN TYPES OF CANCER
Studies have found that exercisers are less likely to get cancer of the colon. Research has also suggested that women who do not exercise have more than two and a half times the risk of developing cancer of the reproductive system and almost twice the chance of getting breast cancer than those who do exercise.

8 CAN SLOW THE AGEING PROCESS
By counterbalancing the natural age-related decrease in work capacity and physical performance, exercise can help you maintain and sustain your ability to perform work and be independent.

9 IMPROVES MENTAL SHARPNESS
Regular exercisers have better memories, better reaction times and a better level of concentration than people who don't exercise.

10 IMPROVES THE QUALITY OF SLEEP
Researchers have found that exercisers go to sleep more quickly, sleep more soundly and are more refreshed in the morning than people who do not exercise. So if you're having trouble sleeping, exercise could well be the answer.

The factors of fitness

The main factors of fitness are generally referred to as the three S's – stamina, suppleness and strength. Only by getting yourself to an adequate level in all three will you attain balanced fitness and optimal wellbeing. I also like to add in a fourth 'S' – skill – something that is often overlooked. The Anyone, Anywhere, Anytime exercise system is ideal as it addresses all four factors. Follow it and you'll end up fitter all round, even if you can only spend a few minutes a day exercising.

Stamina

Building up your stamina so you can sustain exercise for a number of minutes means working to improve the efficiency of your heart, lungs and circulatory system. The exercises that will do this for you are aerobic exercises (see pages 36–37) – those that utilise the large muscle groups of the body, elevate the heart rate, increase body temperature and step up the rate of breathing. Anyone, Anywhere, Anytime gives you dozens of stamina-building aerobic exercises. In addition, other aerobic exercises you can do unsupervised are brisk walking, jogging, cycling, rowing, cross-country skiing, swimming and various non-stop sports such as basketball and squash. Aerobic-type exercise supervised by a qualified instructor, such as circuit training, Tae Bo, Step, Body Pump and Boxercise are other good examples of what you can do to build your stamina.

Suppleness

Suppleness – often referred to as flexibility – is defined as the ability to move a body part through a full range of movement. Limitations to suppleness are commonly caused by tight muscles and tight connective tissue (the ligaments and tendons, see pages 14–15), but these can be improved with correct stretching exercises. Anyone, Anywhere, Anytime will show you how.

Stretching is often overlooked as part of a balanced programme of exercise, especially by men who seem to believe that it might damage their fragile macho egos! However, stretching not only increases your range of movement, it also reduces muscle tension and helps to maintain good posture – all of which is generally beneficial to your health.

Stretching exercises can be tailored to people's needs. For example, runners need to stretch the muscles of the legs and back, while tennis players must stretch the arms, shoulders and midriff.

Strength

Strength is best described as the maximum force a muscle can generate in one effort, whereas muscle stamina is the muscle's ability to contract repeatedly without fatiguing. Strength training plays an important role in helping to control blood pressure, maintain bone mass, prevent injuries and increase the body's metabolism. Using the Anyone, Anywhere, Anytime system regularly, you'll notice a definite increase in your overall strength and you'll see how your body will become more toned.

Skill

Skill – often referred to as 'practice training' – is concerned with making the right decisions and can be improved with repetition. It also depends a little on the other factors of fitness. If you're not strong, then some actions will cause you to strain hard instead of maintaining an easy control. Similarly, a lack of stamina makes skill difficult to achieve. Football is a good example of a game in which a player needs to have a variety of skills at his disposal. It requires good judgement of personal speed, ball speed and eye-to-foot co-ordination. It also requires the player to possess great accuracy when passing the ball or when goal scoring. Anyone, Anywhere, Anytime blends many forms of exercise, so as you progress with it, you'll notice a marked improvement in your overall level of skill as well as in your stamina, suppleness and strength.

BELOW Regular exercise helps achieve that 'picture of good health' look. You just have to make it a priority and go for it.

The body

Before you start any sort of exercise programme, it pays to know something about your body and how it functions. In this section I offer a basic and jargon-free insight into the skeletal and muscular systems as well as into the three different body types. Look at your body objectively and see which type fits best.

The skeletal system

The skeleton consists of 206 bones. Its size and shape are genetically inherited but can be influenced by nutrition and disease. The skeletal system performs the following five basic functions:

1 It provides support for the soft tissues of our bodies and so keeps us erect.

2 **It protects the internal organs of our bodies, such as the brain, heart and lungs.**

3 It provides the surface for the attachment of muscles and serves as a lever for the muscles when movement takes place.

4 **It serves as a storehouse for calcium and phosphorous, which make our bones sturdy and durable.**

5 The red marrow of the bones acts as a chemical laboratory to produce the red blood cells that carry oxygen to the tissues of the body.

Male and female skeletons are similar but with a few slight differences. For example, the bones of a male are thicker and slightly heavier, while women have a wider and shallower pelvis.

Bones contain hard tissue that makes them sturdy and durable, but they are pliable and light enough to permit many types of movement without breaking. Movement occurs at the joints, with the amount of movement depending on the structure and function of the joint. The two basic types of moving joints are ball and socket joints (the hip and shoulder joints) and hinge joints (the elbow joint). Some joints, such as the bones of the skull, permit limited or no movement. The joints that do permit free movement have three characteristics:

1 Between the bones is a space, called the synovial cavity. This contains synovial fluid that helps to lubricate the action of all the moving bones.

2 **An articular cartilage covers the ends of the bones to keep them from rubbing directly on each other.**

3 Dense, tough connective tissues, called ligaments, connect the bones to each other and provide stability to the joints.

The muscular system

The most important organ of the body, the heart, is in fact a muscle, but as well as muscles like this that you can't control, for example the muscles of the blood vessels and digestive system, there are some 650 voluntary – or skeletal – muscles. All muscle is unique amongst the body's organs in that it can increase its performance level by more than 50 times. Skeletal muscles account for about 45 per cent of the body weight of a man and about 36 per cent in women.

The muscular system works with the skeletal system to produce movement and many movements involve the co-ordinated action of a number of muscles. Muscles are attached to the bones by tendons, which are fibrous cords of dense connective tissue. In order to make a movement, muscles have to contract and relax. Flexion of the forearm at the elbow joint, for example, results from contraction of the bicep muscle (front upper arm) and relaxation of the tricep muscle (rear upper arm).

Contraction of the skeletal muscles also helps the body to maintain its posture. Without it, we would fall in a heap. Muscular contractions also produce heat and so help maintain body temperature.

You and your body type

Your best friend makes a beeline for the exercise bike when she needs to fight the flab, but you only have to look at it and your calves turn the size of the Incredible Hulk while your stomach, sadly, stays the same. And your workmate can pig out on cheese sandwiches and chocolate for lunch seven days a week and not put on a gram, but you're bulging over your belt after one plate of fries. Not fair is it? Unfair it may be, but it's all due to your genetic make-up.

Our basic body type sets natural limits to what we can achieve with diet and exercise, but the news isn't all bad. It is possible to redesign (or make the most of) what Mother Nature gave you. Generally speaking, bodies fall into three main categories – Ectomorph, Mesomorph and Endomorph, but very few of us are just one type. Most tend to be a combination. But whatever your dominant shape, the Anyone, Anywhere, Anytime exercise system will help bring out the best in you.

Ectomorph

This body type is usually tall, thin and long-limbed, with slight buttocks, narrow chest and narrow hips. Ectomorphs are generally lean with little body fat and they have a low potential for muscular development. They have fast metabolic rates and remain slim even if they only exercise moderately.

Mesomorph

Mesomorphs are strong, muscular and well-proportioned, with a triangular upper body, slim waist and well-formed legs. They are generally considered to be fine physical specimens, but we can all incline towards this group, which is inspiring and encouraging in itself. Their medium metabolism and small proportion of body fat means they can remain the epitome of physical prowess, as long as they exercise regularly and follow a healthy eating plan.

Endomorph

This body type has a strong, heavy physique, with short limbs, wide waist and hips, and is somewhat round in appearance. A slow metabolism and high proportion of body fat means that endomorphs will almost certainly pile on the kilograms if they don't exercise enough and eat healthily.

Whatever shape you are, the best body shape for you is the one you've inherited from your genetic make-up. How you wear it is up to you, but realistically speaking, you won't develop broad muscular shoulders if you're genetically an ectomorph, or have long, slender limbs if you are a short, rounded endomorph. It's vital to realise that a well-shaped body that's firm and toned, not flabby and fat, doesn't necessarily mean small, thin, petite or slender. Following my Anyone, Anywhere, Anytime exercise system will help you achieve the shape and level of fitness you are comfortable with!

Your body and its functions

In developed countries, over the last half a century there has been a dramatic decline in the amount of physical activity people take. This is a direct result of ever-increasing technological advances both at home and at work. At home we enjoy an array of labour-saving devices that help us cook and clean, and for many of us our leisure time consists of watching television, which turns us into seasoned armchair athletes and couch nature watchers! And at work, many of us don't have to put in the physical effort that was once necessary, while the growth in car use means we all do far less walking than our grandparents did. But humans are designed for mobility and activity so our increasingly sedentary lifestyle has led us to the point where six in every ten people are at risk of developing lifestyle diseases. The main aim of exercise is to help to reverse this trend.

Bodies v. cars

There are similarities between the human body and a car and looking at them can help us understand how the body works. The car, like the body, is not a single unit, but a number of independent parts working in unison. Each part depends on the other to work well, so the car's overall performance will only be as efficient as the weakest part.

We are aware of how important it is that all parts of our car are in good working order, so we have it serviced regularly, yet we often overlook the need to look after our body. But human beings are far more complex than cars, and unlike a car engine, an efficient human engine is about life itself, not just about getting from A to B. An inefficient body will have to overwork to do its job, which means that it simply won't last so long. It also means that we tire more easily. On average, we spend our working day at no more than 40 per cent of our physical maximum, and the less we push ourselves, the more our capacity

drops to the point where even that is enough to make us feel tired at the end of a normal day.

Exercise is the key to increasing our capacity. At times of normal, non-strenuous activity, the average adult's heart beats about 72 times a minute, ejecting around 5,000 millilitres of blood a minute, and approximately 25 per cent of the available oxygen is transferred from the blood to the cells of the body.

During strenuous exercise, things are very different. Our breathing becomes heavier. Our heart rate increases. The amount of blood pumped per beat and the total blood pumped per minute also increase. In fact, from 5,000 millilitres of blood a minute, during heavy exercise the output may reach 25,000 millilitres, so there's a lot more oxygen available for the cells. This ensures they stay healthy and assists in the removal of waste gases from the body.

As you train, your body becomes more efficient at taking oxygen from the blood, so the heart beats more slowly and strongly, doing less work to achieve the same results. And as exercise increases the demand for oxygen from the muscles, so the heart has to pump more and its capacity and efficiency are increased still more. This then has a knock-on effect on your lungs and circulatory and respiratory systems.

Energy sources

Just as a car relies on fuel to get it moving, so our bodies rely on energy, but different activities require different sorts of energy. Fortunately, the body is very good at providing these, mostly from our food.

Our greatest energy fuel is Adenosine Triphosphate (ATP). Some of this is stored in our muscles ready for immediate explosive action, for example dashing for the bus. Unfortunately, muscles only store limited amounts of ATP– enough just to power the first few seconds of really dynamic activity.

Our bodies also have another fuel source which can be converted into ATP – Creatine Phosphate, or PCr. This takes a little longer to kick in, so the energy it produces is slightly less powerful. PCr. enables us to continue fairly explosive effort for roughly another 10 seconds.

A less explosive but more lasting muscle fuel than ATP is glycogen, derived from glucose. This is stored in our muscles and provides an energy supply lasting about 40 seconds.

For lower intensity, longer-term exercise the body utilises its own fat as its main fuel source, but for fat to be drawn on, you need to do aerobic exercise at roughly 65–70 per cent of your maximum intensity.

And so we can see how the body needs different energy sources for different types of activity. If you are a long-distance runner, the main, but not the only, focus of your training will be the aerobic system, while if you are a javelin thrower you will require more short-term energy in the form of ATP, obtained mostly from your food, especially carbohydrates.

DID YOU KNOW?

• It is estimated that in the West, 60 per cent of adults are overweight or obese. The associated health problems can't be ignored, so if you fall into this category – lose weight now!

• **Scientists claim there is an increased risk of certain cancers if your waist measures more than your hips. Measure yours and see. If it does, do something about it now!**

• A person weighing 63 kilograms burns roughly 62 calories per hour while at rest. But if you increase your lean tissue, you'll burn many more calories, even when you're sleeping.

• **Women require fewer calories than men since women have more body fat and fat metabolises more slowly than lean body mass. So, especially for women, the guaranteed way of speeding up your metabolism is to exercise more.**

• An average person's heart at rest beats approximately 72 times per minute, while a fit individual's resting heart rate is around 55 beats per minute. That's a saving of 1,020 beats per hour or a massive saving of 24,480 beats per full day or an incredible 171,360 beats per week or an astronomical 8,910,720 beats saved per year. If you could make this kind of saving on car fuel per year, you'd be running your car on peanuts!

• **Apart from the obvious, the main physical differences between the sexes are:** men have approximately 50 per cent more muscle mass than women as well as greater bone mass; **the female body accumulates approximately 10 per cent more body fat than the male;** the size of an average man's heart is 25 per cent larger than the average woman's and men's lung capacity is about 27 per cent greater than women's.

Understanding drugs

Literally thousands of chemical compounds can be classed as drugs because they change your mental or physical state or function. The body naturally produces some of these, like endorphins – nature's painkillers – and adrenaline, to help us deal with crises. Other drugs, such as caffeine or tobacco derive from plants, while still others, such as penicillin and LSD, are produced in the laboratory. Under normal circumstances, your body regulates its production of these drugs to keep you in a state of equilibrium. But it cannot control the levels of drugs you consume – only you can by deciding whether or not to use legal or illegal drugs.

Illegal drugs

Drug abuse – the use of a drug for non-medicinal purposes – is a huge problem that affects every country in the world and all social strata. People often say they take drugs to feel good or to have fun. One person might have a cigarette at a party, another might smoke pot at a friend's house. Others might take drugs to make them happy when they're depressed, or to help them relax when they're stressed or nervous. By taking drugs, some people think they can be the person they want to be. But the problem with this is that the results aren't real. You haven't changed how you are permanently. You've only made yourself feel better short-term. It's like covering up a big zit on your face. You can't see the zit, but it's still there.

What do drugs do to your body in the short-term?

No matter what your reasons are for taking drugs, your body will suffer. Every drug is different, but they all interfere with the basic functions of your nervous system. Sometimes they affect your muscles too. That's why drug-taking makes people have sensations

they aren't used to – their brains, nerves and muscles have been juggled around.

Besides making you feel different and playing around with the synapses of your brain and your nerves, almost all drugs can make it tougher to sleep. Some also cause major weight gain, some unhealthy weight loss. Your eyes get glassy and bloodshot, your heart races and sometimes you have diarrhoea. Some drugs, such as glue or butane, can even cause immediate death.

There are cosmetic problems too, almost any drug will make your hair and skin less healthy, and many will make you break out in spots – not just on your face, but also on your body.

What do drugs do to your body in the long term?

Long-term effects depend on the drug. For instance, using certain drugs over a long period of time can cause medical problems, ranging from lung cancer to liver problems to big-time brain damage.

Besides these physical effects, drugs can cause major long-term mental health and social problems. Depression can be a serious problem and many

TOP TIPS TO HELP YOU COMBAT DRUGS

If you have a drug problem, there's a lot you can do to help yourself. Begin by considering how bad your drug problem is. Be honest with yourself and seek the objective opinion of people you respect. Most drug abusers think they have more control of their drug use than they actually do. Then:

- **Develop goals for limiting your use of drugs.**
- Develop sub-goals – the methods you will use to achieve each goal (for instance, avoiding social events that may involve drugs, starting an exercise programme, taking up meditation); plan a time frame for starting and completing each sub-goal; create a way of measuring your progress; develop a system of rewards and punishments for success or failure.
- **Write a personal contract with a friend that will help you achieve these goals and will make you feel accountable. Clearly outline your sub-goals, deadlines, rewards and punishments.**
- If your plan fails, don't give up. Get outside help immediately. Waiting will only result in deeper problems.

addicts often end up hurting people, even those they love. They tell lies, steal money, sometimes even get violent. A drug addict's biggest ambition becomes getting high, instead of setting high goals for themselves.

Are drugs always bad?

Take it from me, illegal drugs are always bad. But there are many drugs that were developed as medication to help treat patients with very specific medical conditions, and for those people, drugs make sense. Unfortunately, there are people who use these drugs but who don't need them for medical reasons. Which, if you think about it, is like going for chemotherapy when you don't have cancer!

Why do people keep taking drugs?

Many people don't become addicted to drugs, but may continue to take them for the same reasons they started – because they want to fit in with their friends, because they want to escape from the problems life presents them with, or perhaps because they're bored. These are people who have issues with insecurity, and are scared or unwilling to deal with their problems in a straight-up, intelligent way – by talking to friends, counsellors, even parents!

Other people, for reasons that only the experts can begin to understand, become physically or mentally addicted and eventually, trying to get drugs becomes the most important thing in their lives, using up all their time, money and energy.

Alcohol

If you enjoy a small amount of alcohol, then it's been proved that it's more likely to be beneficial than harmful to you. In fact, according to recent studies, two glasses of red wine each day can even help to guard against heart disease and certain cancers. However, if you're consuming enough alcohol to make a significant contribution to your calorie intake – and that means anything over and above the recommended safe maximum (see page 20) – then you're almost certainly drinking too much!

Excessive drinking over a period of months or years increases the risk of harm to almost every body function, but almost all damage is reversible provided you stop soon enough.

If you don't, these are some of the problems you may eventually face:
• **Liver damage – enlarged liver, fatty liver, jaundice, maybe cirrhosis** • Increased risk of oesophageal and pancreatic cancer • **Inflammation of the stomach** • Deficiency of many nutrients due to loss of interest in food • **Damage to the immune system, resulting in greater susceptibility to infection** • Obesity, with its attendant problems of increased risk of heart attack and diabetes • **Weaker and less regular heartbeat** • High blood pressure, although moderate drinking – up to 2 Units (20ml) of alcohol per day – seems to lower blood pressure! • **Impaired sexual and reproductive function in both sexes** • Short-term effects on the brain – such as impaired judgement, a lowering of inhibitions and loss of balance – and long-term brain and nerve damage

Does alcohol have any nutritional benefits?

Spirits have no nutritional value whatsoever. A glass of wine – red, rosé or white – contains about 15 per cent of the recommended daily allowance (RDA) of iron. A quarter of a litre of ale provides about 10 per cent RDA of the B group vitamins – riboflavin and niacin (see page 31). And that's about it. Unlike most other nutrients, alcohol does not form part of any body structure and is not essential to any of life's chemical processes. The only real nutritional function of alcohol is to provide energy.

How do I measure the amount of alcohol I consume?

The alcohol content of drinks is usually measured as % Vol., or 'alcohol by volume'. If beer is described as having 4% Vol., it's just another way of saying that it contains 4ml of alcohol in every 100ml. So, 250ml would contain 10ml of alcohol. To help make it easier

---

HOW MANY UNITS?

I glass of red wine = 1 Unit
284 ml lager = 1 Unit
1 measure of spirits = 1 Unit
284 ml strong lager or beer = 2 Units

---

to calculate how much you're consuming, it's common to refer to Units of alcohol instead of ml. To convert ml to Units, simply divide by 10. So, the beer in the above example would contain 1 Unit of alcohol.

How much alcohol is sensible?

The medical profession recommends approximately 21 Units a week for a man and 14 for a woman as the safe maximum level. They also suggest that the amount of alcohol that may be taken without harm varies considerably from one person to another.

TIPPLE CONTROL TIPS

• **Do make your own decisions and don't let others persuade you to 'have just one more'.**
• Do take advantage of low-alcohol and alcohol-free drinks.
• **Do eat something before or with an alcoholic drink, but remember that only moderate drinking will ensure that your blood sugar level remains low.**
• Do drink slowly – take sips and put the glass down between sips.
• **Try not to drink alcohol during the working day and certainly don't drink if you work with machinery.**
• Don't drink to quench your thirst – alcohol is dehydrating.

Smoking

If you smoke, then for me to suggest that smoking is not only harmful to your health, but can kill you, may be frowned upon as another overused cliché. But the fact remains, and always will, that smoking poses one of the most lethal threats to your health and your quality of life.

Smoking may still be accepted socially in some pockets of the world, but when it comes to exercising, it's another matter as there is no doubt that smoking severely affects your level of fitness. To start, it suffocates the oxygenated cells when you breathe in, which means that as you struggle to breathe, your exercise sessions become much harder. This then creates a negative effect, making exercise less pleasurable and so undermining your motivation because it all seems too difficult. If you need further convincing of the harmful effects of smoking, just study the list below:

The immediate effects of smoking on your body are:

• **Increases the heart rate** • Increases blood pressure • **Increases hormone production** • Constricts the small blood vessels under the skin • **Produces negative changes in blood composition** • Produces negative changes in metabolism

TOP TIPS TO HELP YOU GIVE UP SMOKING FOREVER

Everyone knows that if you're a smoker, giving up isn't always easy. The key is to plan what you are going to do. The following are some suggestions, from people I know personally who have successfully quit smoking:

• **Decide on the date you are going to quit, and stick to it. Do something special as a treat for the end of the day to reward yourself. But if you're serious about your health and fitness, remember that stuffing yourself with chocolate gateau is not the best reward.**

• Take it one day at a time.

• **Tell your friends and family that you have given up smoking. Your true friends will encourage your abstinence.**

• Change your normal routine slightly. This helps avoid situations that trigger you to smoke.

• **Choose activities to replace smoking and to help distract you (like exercising more!). And whenever you feel a strong urge to smoke, do something else instead. For instance, try some stretching exercises. These encourage deep breathing, which helps to deliver more oxygen to your brain, which in turn will make you feel a whole lot better.**

• When you go out shopping, take just enough money to pay for the essentials, but not enough for a packet of cigarettes.

• **Start a separate, exclusive investment plan with the money you have saved on smoking. Review it every 3 months and watch it grow. Before you know it, you'll have saved enough to treat yourself to a world cruise.**

• Keep at it and whenever you feel you are losing heart, remind yourself why you are giving up smoking and what you are gaining already. Don't be tempted to smoke even a single cigarette as this can easily lead to 2 or 3 and may result in your becoming a smoker again.

• **Think to yourself 'Do I really want to be one of the many hundreds of thousands of victims of lung cancer who die each year?'**

Stress and sleep

Stress can mean tension, a sense of pressure, frustration or an inability to complete a task. It is part of everyday life, but is not always as bad or negative as it may appear. It can help us to achieve higher levels of performance, is essential in keeping us alert and on our toes and can even protect us from possible harmful situations. Without stress, our lives would be monotonous. However, too much stress over a prolonged period of time can have a negative effect on our wellbeing. This is when we may feel we can no longer cope with it – and it becomes distress.

Most stress is triggered by issues at work or in our private lives and these will take time to resolve. But a lot of everyday stress, such as sitting in a traffic jam, or being late for a work meeting, can make us 'blow a fuse'. No matter how tightly you grip the steering wheel, you will still be stuck in that jam. Meanwhile, those pent-up feelings affect you on a physiological level. The body's production of adrenaline increases, which speeds up the heart and the nervous system and increases the blood pressure. It also releases glucose into the bloodstream, which is nature's way of providing the extra energy needed for urgent action.

CORNEL'S TOP COOL-DOWN TIPS

When you're feeling wound-up and stressed-out there's a chance that you could say or do something that you might later regret. Follow my handy tips to help you cool down.

- **Breathe slowly and count to ten.**
- Go outside for a breath of fresh air.
- **When things really get you uptight, give yourself a treat – a cup of tea in the garden, a hot bath, a visit to the shops. The choice is yours.**
- Humour is sometimes the best remedy. If at all possible, try to see the funny side of things.
- **Try to visualise a beautiful, peaceful scene, or whatever your own idea of paradise is.**
- Plan your day in advance so you won't feel too pressured – but try to keep cool if things don't go according to plan.
- **Write down the things that seem to be the cause of your stress and then deal with them one at a time.**
- Take a break. A short holiday, a day off or just a walk in the park can break your routine and lower your stress levels.
- **If you drink or smoke to unwind, try cutting down. Drinking or smoking won't solve the problems that are making you tense.**
- Have a massage. This will help to unknot tense bits of your body.
- **Finally, do some exercise. After a stressful day you may just want to slump in front of the television, but a bit of exercise will help you unwind, make you feel better and will bring you health benefits too.**

Who is prone to stress?

Almost anyone can suffer from stress – company executives, housewives, policemen or secretaries – all are equally susceptible. It's simply part of modern life, but whether we suffer from it or not depends on our reaction to it. Often those who are very hard-working or are always ready to take up any type of challenge get the most stressed and it's these people especially who need to adopt a more relaxed attitude to life.

Sleep

When you sleep, your body relaxes totally and you should wake up feeling refreshed and recharged. A good night's sleep can help you recover from the stresses of yesterday, and give you enough energy to cope with the stresses of the day to come, while lack of sleep can result in impaired concentration, added stress and a lowering of the body's natural defences against illness.

On average, most of us sleep for about eight hours a night, but it's the quality of our sleep rather than the quantity that's important. And as you age, your ability to sleep at night diminishes. This is partly caused by a reduction in the melatonin levels in your body – the hormone associated with sleep. Melatonin supplements are widely available and are useful for treating short-term sleep deprivation, but I advise against them as they have unwanted side effects. Instead, whatever your age, I recommend regular exercise as the most effective way to maximise your body's production of melatonin.

CORNEL'S TOP 10 TIPS FOR A GOOD NIGHT'S REST

Many people have great difficulty in falling asleep and staying asleep. If you have trouble sleeping, try some or all of my tips for a good night's rest.

1 Try a traditional cure for insomnia. A hot bath will increase the blood flow to your skin and make you sleepy, while a drink of milk contains tryptophan, a substance that helps you sleep.

2 Stay away from alcohol, coffee, cigarettes and heavy meals before going to bed as they can cause sleeplessness later in the night.

3 Respect your natural sleep cycle by establishing a schedule and not varying it. Ideally you need to go to sleep and wake at the same time each day.

4 Start to do relaxing and calming things an hour or so before you go to bed.

5 Make the bedroom more conducive to sleep. Light-excluding blinds or curtains, a new pillow or a better-quality mattress may all help.

6 Try a little guided imagery to help you relax. Imagine yourself on a tropical beach. Feel the sun and sand against your skin. Hear the waves lapping at the shore.

7 Do not clutter your bedroom with too many electrical items as this can lead to electromagnetic stress.

8 Avoid reading or watching anything on television that may get you too excited or anxious just before you go to bed.

9 Try lying in bed and breathing deeply for a count of 10, then exhaling for a count of 15, ensuring you expel all the air from your lungs. This will help you to relax and should make you fall asleep more quickly.

10 Finally, exercise, but do it earlier on in the day rather than just before bed or it will interfere with your night's sleep.

Eating for fitness

Eating for good health and dieting are the subjects of much debate in today's society. Arguably, food and nutrition have become modern-day obsessions, to the point where it seems there are more diets around than there are food recipes. The whole issue can be terribly confusing. You'll find advice on what to eat and what not to eat in every magazine and newspaper, on television, on radio and of course, among your friends. You'll probably know at least a couple of people who are on a diet at this very moment. You may at some stage of your life have followed a diet programme of some description or have considered it.

Extensive research during the last few decades has made us more aware of the effects of diet and exercise on our health. Today we recognise that poor nutrition and bad eating habits can contribute to lack of fitness, low energy levels, and the development of lifestyle diseases such as obesity, cardiovascular disease, certain cancers, diabetes and osteoporosis. We now realise that, to some extent, we really are what we eat. And, as I've already said, in some ways, what petrol is to your car, food is to your body. Without food you will not function, you will have no energy. And just as a car needs the right type of petrol, so your body will perform better with the right foods.

In general, the secret of a good eating programme is balance. Your body requires a wide spectrum of nutrients and these can only be gained through eating a range of the correct foods in appropriate quantities. So the time has come for you to start making wise food choices as well as committing to a regular fitness programme. These two strategies combined are the most effective means of enhancing your health and feelings of wellbeing. To start with, let's learn a little about the different nutrients, where to find them and what role each one plays.

The seven nutrient categories

Food basically consists of seven categories of nutrients, each with its own set of vital functions.

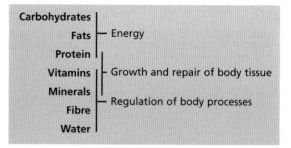

Carbohydrates
Fats — Energy
Protein
Vitamins — Growth and repair of body tissue
Minerals
Fibre — Regulation of body processes
Water

Energy is made available in our bodies by the breaking down of the nutrients in the foods we eat into their basic 'building blocks'. As you can see, carbohydrates, fats and protein – the macronutrients – supply energy. Carbohydrates break down into monosaccharides, fats break down into fatty acids, and protein breaks down into amino acids.

Vitamins, minerals and fibre – the micronutrients– only provide minute amounts of energy, but vitamins and minerals play an important role in the transfer of energy from carbohydrates, fats and protein.

CORNEL'S TOP 10 FOOD MYTHS AND FACTS

1 **MYTH** Eating fat is bad for you.
FACT Saturated fat – the kind that is found in fatty meat, pastries and cakes – is the baddie. But unsaturated fats found in fish and vegetables are good for you.

2 **MYTH** You should abstain from shellfish because it contains high levels of cholesterol and we all know this is bad for you.
FACT Prawns, crab and lobster all contain cholesterol, but they are also high in essential fatty acids which help protect the heart.

3 **MYTH** Eating carbohydrates and protein at the same time is bad for you.
FACT Our stomachs are designed to deal with whatever we consume, breaking it up with the acids it secretes. The reason why non-food combining diets – the sort that limit you to just one food type at a meal – work is that most people find meals of this sort so boring that they invariably end up eating less. Why don't you try it for yourself and see?

4 **MYTH** Honey is healthier than sugar.
FACT The problem is, both are high in calories. A level teaspoonful of honey contains 20 calories and the equivalent amount of sugar contains 17. So both should be avoided, although honey does have some healing properties.

5 **MYTH** Red meat causes heart disease.
FACT Red meat does not cause heart disease – it's the fat in it that's dangerous. You can continue enjoying steaks, but be sure to trim off all visible fat and grill instead of fry. Better still, buy lean mince and drain the fat well when you cook it. Calorie-wise, red meat is slightly more calorific than white, but not much.

6 **MYTH** Anything containing bran must be good for you.
FACT Oat bran may help lower cholesterol, but you'd have to eat it in large quantities to receive the benefits. And research has shown that the phytic acid in bran prevents the body from absorbing certain vitamins that are vital for healthy skin, hair and hormone production.

7 **MYTH** Fast food is more fattening than normal home cooking.
FACT Not necessarily. A large fast-food hamburger contains about 550 calories, but a home-made burger could have as many as 800 calories – and more if you use fatty meat and pile on the mayonnaise and ketchup.

8 **MYTH** Eat low-fat foods and you'll lose weight.
FACT Maybe, but what about sugary foods and alcohol? Both contain no fat, but are loaded with calories. Be on your guard when you purchase so-called low-fat foods. Some are packed with sugar to compensate for the lack of fat that gives flavour. What matters is the total calorie content of the food you eat.

9 **MYTH** Eating yoghurt makes you live longer.
FACT There is no scientific proof of this, but yoghurt makes a great dessert if your goal is to lose weight. It is relatively low in calories (about 50 calories for a carton of low-fat yoghurt) and contains valuable calcium and protein.

10 **MYTH** Bread and potatoes will make you fat.
FACT Starchy foods are actually lower in calories than fatty ones and contain essential nutrients for overall wellbeing. It's the high-fat spreads we put on our bread and the butter we add to potatoes that make us fat.

THE BASICS OF FITNESS

YOU ARE WHAT YOU EAT

The following questionnaire will help you to determine whether your daily eating habits are good for management of your weight. It will also help you identify changes that you may need to make. Simply circle the appropriate number in response to each question. (You may wish to do this on a photocopy of the page.) Use the following guidelines to help you answer:

RARELY – almost never   SOMETIMES – once or twice a week   OFTEN – four or more times a week

HOW OFTEN DO YOU:

1 Eat fried foods rather than foods which are baked, grilled or boiled?
3 Rarely 2 Sometimes 1 Often

2 Consume a nutritious breakfast?
1 Rarely 2 Sometimes 3 Often

3 Opt for low-fat or non-fat foods?
1 Rarely 2 Sometimes 3 Often

4 Plan ahead of time for your meals?
1 Rarely 2 Sometimes 3 Often

5 Skip meals?
3 Rarely 2 Sometimes 1 Often

6 Overeat and wish that you had not eaten so much?
3 Rarely 2 Sometimes 1 Often

7 Eat at fast food restaurants because you do not have time to sit down and relax and enjoy a quiet, leisurely meal?
3 Rarely 2 Sometimes 1 Often

8 Get up in time so that you can eat breakfast at home?
1 Rarely 2 Sometimes 3 Often

9 Crave for a dessert after eating an adequate meal?
3 Rarely 2 Sometimes 1 Often

10 Purchase unhealthy, fattening foods, such as chips, ice cream, cookies, etc?
3 Rarely 2 Sometimes 1 Often

11 Eat in one main place when eating at home?
1 Rarely 2 Sometimes 3 Often

12 Engage in other activities, such as watching TV or reading while eating?
3 Rarely 2 Sometimes 1 Often

13 Avoid the negative influence of friends and peers on your eating habits?
1 Rarely 2 Sometimes 3 Often

14 Take 20 minutes or longer to eat your meals?
1 Rarely 2 Sometimes 3 Often

15 Take part in regular exercise?
1 Rarely 2 Sometimes 3 Often

16 Leave food on your plate?
1 Rarely 2 Sometimes 3 Often

17 Drink at least 6–8 glasses of water daily?
1 Rarely 2 Sometimes 3 Often

18 Drink more than 2 alcoholic drinks daily?
3 Rarely 2 Sometimes 1 Often

19 Drink at least one glass of water or other low calorie fluid before each meal?
1 Rarely 2 Sometimes 3 Often

20 Eat in response to something other than hunger?
3 Rarely 2 Sometimes 1 Often

Now add together the numbers that you circled to make your grand total.

Record your score here _____

HOW DID YOU SCORE?
20–36 Very poor. Your eating habits need a lot of attention.

37–47 Average. You are doing all right, but there is room for improvement.

48–60 Very good. You have developed good, consistent habits. However, do not reward yourself by overeating.

Carbohydrates

Not so long ago carbohydrates were frowned on but we now realise their importance. They are your body's primary energy source, they serve to ensure that your brain and nervous system function properly, and they help your body use fat more efficiently.

Stored carbohydrates (glycogen) are the main fuel for activity. If you're having difficulty maintaining your energy levels during an exercise session, it may indicate that you have inadequate levels of glycogen. Unless these levels are restored, your exercise session will continue to deteriorate, resulting in fatigue.

At least 55–60 per cent of our daily calorie consumption should come from carbohydrates. However, much of this should come from the complex carbohydrates such as cereals, rice, pulses, pasta, bread and vegetables. Unfortunately, most of us tend to consume more of the simple carbohydrates in the form of sugary foods, such as biscuits, sweets, chocolates and fizzy drinks.

Fats

Fat is today's dirty word, but you must understand the difference between dietary fat and body fat. Dietary fat is the fat we consume – cream, oil, butter and cheese. When you eat too much, it is stored in the body where it encourages cardiovascular problems and is directly linked to excess weight.

Which brings us to the subject of body fat. This is caused by excess food of any type that you've eaten. It has been broken down by the body into its 'building blocks' but has not been used up. Instead, it is stored in your body's fat cells.

There are some essential fats which are as important to us as other nutrients, but you only need a small amount. However, almost without exception, the majority of us eat far too much fat, often without realising it because most fatty foods taste so good!

Generally speaking, most of us would benefit from eating 28 grams less each day. This doesn't sound a great deal, and it isn't. Minor changes in what we choose to eat can often do the trick.

The fat found in most food is a mixture of two types: saturates and unsaturates. Unsaturates can be further divided into monounsaturates and polyunsaturates. The difference between these types of fat is their chemical make-up.

Some unsaturates are necessary in small quantities for good health. Good sources are vegetable oils such as sunflower, corn, soya, rapeseed and olive oils, soft margarine labelled 'high in polyunsaturates', nuts and most oily fish. Fats that are hard tend to contain the most saturates. It is these that increase the level of cholesterol in your blood and raise the risk of heart disease. Obviously, they are best kept to a minimum. The richest sources of saturates are commonly found in cooking fats, butter, cakes, biscuits, cheese, some savoury snacks and chocolate. You should limit your fat intake to just 25 per cent of your daily calories and ensure they mostly come from unsaturated fats.

Protein

Protein is broken down into amino acids during digestion and these are used by the body to build, repair and maintain muscle tissue. There are essential and non-essential amino acids; protein that contains all the essential ones is called 'complete protein'. Examples of complete protein are meat, fish, milk, eggs and various vegetables products, such as soybeans. Protein intake recommendations vary according to the individual. For someone leading a normal lifestyle, 0.75 of a gram per kilogram of body weight is adequate, whereas a very active person or regular exerciser would require about double this amount, or approximately 15–18 per cent of their total daily calorie intake.

Vitamins and minerals

Vitamins are organic substances and minerals are inorganic. Your body requires both in minute quantities. They act as catalysts – substances that help trigger other reactions in the body – and also play a part in a variety of metabolic processes.

Vitamins are divided into two classifications: fat-soluble and water-soluble. This gives a clue as to why your body can store some vitamins yet needs others daily. Vitamins such as A, D, E and K dissolve in fat and so can accumulate in our fat tissues, while those that dissolve in water are excreted. These are the ones we need to replace.

Minerals are involved in body structures and work alongside vitamins to make the body function correctly. They are divided into two groups: macronutrients, of which your body requires more than 100 milligrams a day, and micronutrients, trace nutrients, of which you need no more than a few milligrams daily. Most minerals cannot be stored in the body for long periods and are excreted daily.

By varying your food consumption and including plenty of fruit and vegetables, you can obtain all the vitamins and minerals your body needs. But to ensure that the foods you eat are as nutritious as possible, they should be fresh or properly stored, otherwise they will lose some of their nutrient content. You can eat convenience foods as an alternative to fresh, provided you are selective. Frozen, dried, chilled or fortified foods can provide as good a source of vitamins and minerals as fresh foods.

Some people take regular vitamin and mineral supplements, but this is not normally necessary as most of these nutrients are present in your food. However, supplements may be advised in certain circumstances. For instance, women who have heavy periods may need extra iron; women who are planning to become pregnant should take folic acid tablets until they are 12 weeks pregnant, and athletes who train hard may feel the need to take supplements as an 'insurance' against vitamin and mineral deficiency. The required amount of each of these vital nutrients varies and is set out in internationally recognised guidelines (the 'recommended daily allowance' or RDA) commonly found on food packaging.

It is equally important to understand that excessive intake of these vital nutrients can be extremely toxic. Fortunately, it is very unlikely that someone reaches toxic levels through food alone.

Fibre

Fibre is a type of carbohydrate made up of a number of complex substances found only in plants. We should all aim to eat more fibre-rich foods as they stimulate the digestive system, help prevent constipation, make us feel full and help reduce the risk of digestive disorders. They also contain few calories. However, fibre-rich foods, such as wholemeal bread, pasta, pulses and potatoes, provide more than just fibre. They are also rich in protein, complex carbohydrates, vitamins and minerals. It is recommended that we eat 18 grams of fibre daily.

Water

Water is often overlooked as a vital nutrient, but it is very important and accounts for about 80 per cent of our total body weight. It acts as a means of transportation for the various chemicals in the body. For many of us our main source of fluid is sweet fizzy drinks, tea and coffee, and we consume inadequate amounts of water. Yet you should be aiming to consume at least 1.5 litres or more of plain water daily. And don't worry, you can never get fat on water. It yields zero calories. Yes, you may experience a temporary weight increase, but your body will rid itself of any excess fluid when nature calls!

ABOUT LOSING WEIGHT

We are constantly bombarded by the media with exhortations to lose weight. With the entire multi-million pound slimming industry ready and willing to help us spend our money, there is no shortage of diets and weight-loss products around. Yet levels of obesity in Western society have increased beyond belief and continue to do so. Being overweight is now an epidemic, as regular reports in the newspapers tell us.

But more often than not we tend to think of dieting as meaning only one thing – weight loss. Most of us don't really care where the weight loss occurs or how it occurs, so long as it shows as a minus figure on the bathroom scales. But the truth is, it's extremely important from where and how you lose weight. The purpose of weight loss is to rid your body of excess, unhealthy fat. It is not to lose body muscle.

Overweight people can happily lose weight when they keep strictly to a diet. Typically, almost all women who go on a 1200-calorie-a-day diet lose more than 5 kilos in 6 months. Follow up those same women a year later though, and only half will have maintained their weight loss, while 5 years later, the figure falls to a miserable 1 in 10.

That's not to say that calorie counting is not an essential part of weight management. It is. But the simple plain fact is that if you consume more calories than you need, you will get fat. Conversely, if you eat fewer calories than you need, you will definitely lose weight.

On average, women need approximately 2000 calories a day and men about 2500 calories to maintain their body weight. But different people need different amounts of energy to do the same amount of work, so what really matters is the amount of energy you, as an individual, need to maintain the status quo.

That is why no special diet – the sort of crash diet promoted in the media – will work for you long term. It can and will work – and will often on occasion seem like a miracle – but in the short-term only. It may seem to help to kick-start your weight loss. You'll feel like a new person, well on track to your ideal figure. But the fact is, your body will rebel against this kind of dieting in a number of ways you may not be aware of.

Firstly, eating so little means feeling hungry, listless and possibly faint, so it is difficult to sustain a very restrictive diet for long. Secondly, it means the body is unlikely to be adequately nourished as such small quantities of food can't possibly provide enough nutrients for wellbeing. Thirdly, rapid weight loss involves losing essential muscle and fluids as well as some fat. So, although you may be lighter on your bathroom scales, you have in effect lost little fat! Lastly, your metabolic rate slows down and it becomes even harder to lose weight.

So although we live in an age of instant gratification, when it comes to the battle of the bulge, regular exercise and avoiding a high-fat diet are the real ways to victory.

Foods to supply your vitamins and minerals

Almost all food contains some vitamins and minerals, but to make the most of these essential nutrients they should be eaten as fresh as possible. They are only needed in relatively small quantities, but if we don't have them our bodies begin to malfunction and their absence can cause major deficiency symptoms. Medical science is only just beginning to discover exactly how these nutrients work, but each discovery suggests they play an important role in almost all our body functions. Most vitamins and minerals cannot be produced by our bodies, so it's crucial that we include them in a healthy, well-balanced diet. To meet your daily requirements you should aim for maximum variety in your eating habits. The tables on the following pages set out the main food sources and functions of both fat- and water-soluble vitamins and the macro- and micronutrient minerals.

FAT-SOLUBLE VITAMINS	MAIN FOOD SOURCES	MAIN FUNCTIONS
Vitamin A (Retinol)	Liver, dairy products (not low-fat), butter/margarine, green leafy vegetables, yellow vegetables and fruit	Essential for normal growth and development; essential to prevent 'night blindness'; maintenance of surface cells such as the skin and the lining of the gut
Vitamin D (Calciferol)	Eggs, butter, liver, fish oil, fortified margarine (also manufactured in the body by the action of sunlight on the skin)	Growth and mineralisation of the bones; aids in absorption of calcium and phosphorous from food
Vitamin E (Alpha-tocopherol)	Wheatgerm, vegetable oils/margarine, nuts, wholegrain products, green leafy vegetables	Red blood cell production; acts as an antioxidant, so may protect cell membranes
Vitamin K	Liver, meat, green leafy vegetables, soya beans, cauliflower, cabbage	Important in the blood-clotting mechanism; functioning of some bone and kidney proteins

WATER-SOLUBLE VITAMIN	MAIN FOOD SOURCES	MAIN FUNCTIONS
Vitamin C (Ascorbic acid)	Green leafy vegetables, parsley and capsicum, citrus fruits, currants, berries, tropical fruits and tomatoes	Maintenance of connective tissue, cartilage tendons and bone; facilitates absorption of iron; helps in wound healing and muscle regeneration; protects against oxidants
Vitamin B1 (Thiamin)	Meat (especially pork), yeast, whole grains, nuts, all vegetables	Energy production through carbohydrate metabolism and so helps nerve and heart function
Vitamin B2 (Riboflavin)	Milk and milk products, yeast, organ meats, eggs, whole grains, green leafy vegetables	Energy production through fat and protein metabolism; necessary for growth and development
Niacine (Nicotinic acid)	Meat, liver, fish, eggs, yeast, some green leafy vegetables, peanuts, wholegrain products	A vital component of co-enzymes concerned with energy processes
Vitamin B6 (Pyridoxine)	Mainly high-protein products, whole grains, yeast, cereals, vegetables, peanuts, bananas	Has a role in protein metabolism and glucose metabolism.
Vitamin B12 (Cobalamin)	Liver, meat, dairy products, oysters, sardines	Formation of genetic materials; development of red blood cells
Folic acid	Liver, meat, fish, green leafy vegetables, orange juice	Formation of genetic materials; maintenance of normal red blood cell production
Pantothenic acid	Meat, poultry, fish, grains, cereals, legumes, yeast, egg yolk	Central role in carbohydrate, fat and protein metabolism

MACRONUTRIENT MINERAL	MAIN FOOD SOURCES	MAIN FUNCTIONS
Calcium	Milk, cheese, yoghurt, green leafy vegetables	Bone structure, blood clotting; transmission of nerve impulses; muscle contraction
Chlorine	Common table salt	Maintenance of electrolyte and fluid balance
Magnesium	Most foods, especially wholegrain products, green leafy vegetables, fruits and other vegetables	Involved in the regulation of protein, muscle contraction and body temperature; essential for helping with regulation in energy production
Phosphorus	Milk, poultry, fish, meat	Formation of bones and teeth (with calcium); essential to the normal functioning of B group vitamins; important role in the final delivery of energy to all cells, including muscle, in the form of ATP (see energy sources, page 17)
Potassium	Abundant in most foods, especially meat, fish, poultry, cereals, oranges, bananas, fresh vegetables	Muscle function; nerve transmission; carbohydrate and protein metabolism; maintenance of body fluids and the acid base balance of the blood
Sodium	Table salt, soy sauce, seafoods, dairy products, processed foods, yeast spreads	Extremely important co-role with potassium to help to carry out the functions mentioned above

MICRONUTRIENT MINERAL	MAIN FOOD SOURCES	MAIN FUNCTIONS
Chromium	Traces in meat and vegetables	Functions with insulin to help control glucose metabolism
Cobalt	Meat, liver, milk, green leafy vegetables	Component of vitamin B12 may help prevent anaemia and nervous system disorders
Copper	Meat, vegetables, fish, oysters, drinking water from copper pipes	Component of many enzymes; role in haemoglobin formation
Fluorine	In water supplies, tea, some small fish	Prevention of tooth decay; possible role in prevention of osteoporosis
Iodine	Iodised salt, seafood	Component of thyroid hormones that regulate metabolic rate
Iron	Liver, heart, lean red meat, dried apricots, kidney beans, green leafy vegetables	Formation of components essential to the transportation and utilisation of oxygen
Manganese	Wholegrain cereal, green leafy vegetables, wheatgerm, nuts, bananas	Involvement of bone structure and nervous system activity; co-factor in carbohydrate metabolism
Selenium	Mainly protein foods, wholegrain products	Component of an anti-oxidant enzyme helping to protect cells from oxidation by 'free radicals'
Zinc	Meat, eggs, liver, oysters, wholegrain products, legumes	Component of many enzymes; aids wound healing; growth co-factor in protein and carbohydrate metabolism
Cadmium, nickel, silicon, tin, vanadium	Most animal and plant foods	Still undergoing scientific research

My sensible eating plan

Over a period of years I've devised what I view as a simple, sensible eating plan. It's non-restrictive, provides plenty of choices and is easy to follow. It's not a diet, but a guide to the different food types and groups. Many of the clients I've trained have used it very successfully, so why not give it a try yourself? You should aim to eat the foods listed in the Eat Regularly column, every day if possible. Those in the Eat in Moderation column you should only have in moderate amounts 2–3 times a week, and the Try to Avoid foods – well, that's self-explanatory.

	EAT REGULARLY	EAT IN MODERATION	TRY TO AVOID
Cereal foods	Wholemeal flour and bread, porridge oats, crispbreads, brown rice, wholemeal pasta	White bread, white rice and pasta, plain semi-sweet biscuits, muesli.	Sweet biscuits, cream-filled biscuits, cream crackers, cheese biscuits, croissants
Fruit and vegetables	All fresh, frozen, dried and unsweetened tinned fruit; all fresh, frozen, dried and tinned vegetables (especially peas, baked beans, broad beans, lentils and baked potatoes, including the skin)	Fruit in syrup, avocado, olives, roast potatoes cooked in suitable oil, reduced-fat oven chips	Deep-fat fried chips
Fish	All fresh and frozen fish, e.g. cod, plaice, herring, mackerel, plus canned fish in brine or tomato sauce e.g. sardines and tuna	Prawns, lobster, crab, tinned fish in oil (drained)	Fish roe, taramasalata, fried scampi
Meat	Chicken, turkey (without the skin), veal, soya protein meat substitute	Lean beef, pork, lamb, ham, gammon, very lean minced meat, liver, kidney, grilled back bacon	Sausages, luncheon meat, corned beef, pâté, salami, streaky bacon, duck, goose, meat pies and pasties, scotch eggs, visible fat on meats, crackling, chicken skin
Eggs and dairy foods	Skimmed milk, soya milk, powdered skimmed milk, cottage cheese, low-fat curd cheese, low-fat yoghurt, low-fat fromage frais	Semi-skimmed milk, eggs, medium fat cheeses, e.g. Edam, Camembert, Gouda, Brie, cheese spreads, cheeses labelled 'low-fat'	Whole milk and cream, full-fat yoghurt, evaporated or condensed milk, high-fat cheese, e.g. Stilton, Cheddar, cream cheese

	EAT REGULARLY	EAT IN MODERATION	TRY TO AVOID
Fats	Small amounts only	Margarine labelled 'high in poly-unsaturates' or 'high in monounsaturates; low-fat spreads, corn oil, sunflower oil, soya oil, olive oil	All margarines, shortenings and oils not labelled 'high in polyunsaturates' or 'high in mono-unsaturates', butter, lard, suet and dripping, all spreads not labelled 'low-fat'
Prepared foods	Jelly (low-sugar), sorbet, fat-free homemade soups, low- fat, low-sugar yoghurt, low-fat natural yoghurt, low-fat frozen yoghurt	Pastry, puddings, cakes, biscuits, sauces, etc. made with wholemeal flour and fat or oil as above	Pastries, puddings, cakes and sauces made with whole milk and fat or oil as above, suet dumplings or puddings, cream soups
Sweets, jams, spreads and snacks	Marmite, Bovril, chutneys and pickles, sugar-free artificial sweeteners, walnuts and chestnuts	Fish and meat pastes, peanut butter, low-sugar jams and marmalades, other nuts, boiled sweets, fruit pastilles, jellies, honey	Chocolate spreads, chocolate toffees, fudge, butterscotch, ice cream, coconut, crisps and savoury snacks
Drinks	Freshly made tea, coffee (not too many, not too strong!), mineral water, fruit juices (unsweetened)	Alcohol, sweetened drinks, squashes, fruit juice, malted milk or hot chocolate drinks made with skimmed milk	Whole-milk drinks, cream-based liqueurs
Sauces and dressings	Herbs, spices, Tabasco sauce, Worcestershire sauce, soy sauce, lemon juice	Homemade dressings and mayonnaise made with suitable oil, salad dressing made with suitable fat or oil, 'low-fat' or 'low-calorie' mayonnaises and dressings, Parmesan cheese	Ordinary or cream dressings and mayonnaises, salad dressing or mayonnaise made with unsuitable oil

Note: *If you are overweight, foods high in sugar should be avoided and you should strictly limit your intake of allowed fats and oils*

My checklist for healthy eating

- Arm yourself by increasing your knowledge of food
- Eat a variety of different foods
- Reduce your fat intake
- Beware of your sugar intake
- Drastically reduce salt intake
- Drink at least 1.5 litres of plain filtered or bottled water daily
- Consume at least 5 or more portions of fruit and vegetables
- Eat plenty of foods rich in complex carbohydrates
- Eat smaller food portions at each meal
- Consume no more than 2 alcoholic beverages daily – preferably red wine
- And finally, enjoy your food

Aerobic exercise

Aerobic exercise involves increasing your aerobic capacity, which means placing a demand on your cardiovascular system – the heart and blood vessels. It's an essential part of your exercise programme if you want to burn off excess body fat. Ideally, you should be aiming to exercise 3 or 4 times a week at the correct level of intensity for 15–30 minutes, but I know that many people are really short of time, so on the basis that 'every little helps' I offer plenty of useful tips on essential exercises for when you're short of time.

THE KEY POINTS OF AEROBIC EXERCISE

1 The word aerobic means 'with oxygen'.

2 The heart is at the centre of the cardiovascular system and is responsible for pumping oxygen through the blood to the muscles.

3 Regular aerobic exercise is the key to improving the efficiency of the heart and lungs.

4 Other benefits of aerobic exercise include weight/fat loss, decreased cholesterol levels and increased energy.

Exercise intensity

To maximise the benefits of exercising, it's important that you exercise intensively enough and don't give up as soon as the going gets tough. For your aerobic exercise to be effective, your heart rate should ideally be maintained at a level between 65 and 85 per cent of your maximum. This is known as your 'aerobic training zone' and varies according to your physical condition and age. First you need to find your aerobic training zone in the chart opposite.

Now you need to find your resting heart rate. The easiest way to do this is by placing your index and middle fingers on the inside of your wrist at the radial artery or by using the same fingers to press the left side of your neck on your jugular vein. You will be able to feel your pulse. Use a watch or clock with a second hand or counter, and count your pulse for 6 seconds, then multiply the result by 10 to find the rate per minute. For example, if your 6-second heartbeat count is 14, your heart rate is 140 beats per minute. When you exercise, you'll need to get this rate up to your training zone rate. After a bit of practice, you'll be able to use this pulse method even while you are exercising.

As an alternative, you might want to invest in a heart-rate monitor, which will remove the tedium of checking your pulse rate manually. I find these monitors invaluable. They are accurate and durable, but they're not cheap. They consist of a multifunction watch that acts as the monitor, and a chest harness that transmits your heart signal to the watch, so you get a real-time readout of your heart rate. Like a good stocks and share tip, I recommend this as a 'Buy'.

Build it up

During the first few months of your exercise programme, it is advisable to keep your heart rate near the low end of your training zone as you exercise. After a few months, you should gradually aim to increase your heart rate until it is near the middle of your training zone.

As you continue to exercise, you will probably notice that your resting heart rate will become lower on average. You will also notice that you may need to work yourself a little harder to increase your heart rate within your training parameters. This indicates that your cardiovascular system is working more efficiently and you are experiencing the positive effects of aerobic training that I've described on pages 16–17.

RIGHT Checking the pulse at the radial artery is reliable.

FIND YOUR AEROBIC TRAINING ZONE

Age	Newcomer and Restarter aerobic training zone (heartbeats per minute)	Regular and Vigorous aerobic training zone (heartbeats per minute)
20	133–162	138–167
25	132–160	136–166
30	130–158	135–164
35	129–156	134–162
40	127–155	132–161
45	125–153	131–159
50	124–150	129–156
55	122–149	127–155
60	121–147	126–153
65	119–145	125–151
70	118–144	123–150

Muscle conditioning

Contrary to popular belief, muscle conditioning need not mean adding balloon-sized arms and legs to your frame. It is a popular and important component of a well-balanced fitness programme. Not only does it help to build strength, it also carries other benefits, such as increasing your bone density and so helping to prevent injury, toning and shaping your body to improve your physical appearance, and increasing your metabolic rate. Simply put, this means making your body burn more calories per hour, even while sleeping!

That's why I've included six toning, or muscle-conditioning, exercises for each of the exercise types in Anyone, Anywhere, Anytime. Each one focuses on a different body part – typically those that people are most concerned about. If you're short of time and can't do your aerobic circuit as well as your toning exercises, you could just do the toning exercises, and still get some benefit. And if you're even more short of time, why not just choose the toning exercise for the bit of your body that you're least satisfied with? As I always say, every little helps.

To build strength and tone and shape, your muscles must be 'overloaded', or worked beyond their normal level. This overloading creates tiny microtears in your muscle tissue. After a while, the muscles rebuild so they're stronger and more toned than before.

BELOW Isometric exercise doesn't require any equipment.

There are three types of training forms that improve the strength and tone of our muscles. Some require the use of equipment, but since my aim in Anyone, Anywhere, Anytime is to ensure that you can exercise anywhere, without the need for special home equipment or visits to the gym, my suggested toning programmes concentrate mainly on isotonic exercise complemented by some isometric exercises.

Isometric

This type of training is commonly known as 'static contraction' exercises. They consist of contracting and holding a muscle in a fixed or steady position. Examples are the pelvic tilt and the popular static squat and hold against a wall.

Isotonic

This type of training is commonly associated with training with weights and involves moving a body part throughout a range of motion. The result is that the muscles are repeatedly shortened and lengthened.

Isokinetic

This works on a training principle known as 'accommodating resistance', and it requires the use of special equipment. Effectively, the force caused by the speed or intensity of each individual muscle contraction automatically adjusts the resistance. The result is that pushing slowly on the machine means a lower intensity level, whereas pressing harder means heavier resistance. But not everyone has access to special equipment. With Triple A you can do without – so no trips to the gym when you're not in the mood!

RIGHT Working with dumbbells is isotonic exercise.

Clothing and equipment

Kitting yourself out for exercise need not be an excuse for a fashion show, but many of us choose our workout wear for looks and branding, rather than for comfort and practicality. It pays to remember that, whatever you wear, you're going to end up looking like a sweaty strawberry, so you may as well be a comfortable sweaty strawberry!

There are two possible approaches to buying your workout wear. On the basis that by following my Anyone, Anywhere, Anytime programme your body shape will change for the better, you may prefer to buy from one of the cheaper ranges to begin with. But I usually suggest buying the best you can afford, particularly if you're planning to exercise at least three times a week, and making sure what you buy washes well (you may need two sets). Spending that little extra on better quality workout wear may, over time, prove more economical. And if you're a woman, it's essential to have a comfortable, supporting sports bra.

Training shoes

These are perhaps the most crucial item of clothing. Getting them right makes the difference between injury-free exercise and aching joints and blisters. A trip to your local sports shop will reveal a huge array of shoes – for tennis, squash, running, and so on. It can all be very confusing, but I recommend you buy a pair of all-purpose cross trainers.

The next thing to consider is how much you want to spend. If you have good exercise intentions (and I'm assuming you do!) and are planning to workout daily, then a low-budget pair of shoes probably won't last too long. Of course, you can't spend more than you can afford, but some people begrudge spending a lot on training shoes, but wouldn't think twice about spending a similar sum on a pair of toe-crushing, ankle-breaking fashion shoes! The best thing is to go for mid-price shoes that won't break the bank, but won't ruin your feet either. Above all, they should be comfortable and should fit correctly, and I always suggest that, the more black in the shoe, the better. Running or walking in damp, muddy conditions will play havoc with your gleaming white trainers.

Of course, you can save money if you buy in the sales. Discounts can be very generous then, as the retailers need to make space to stock the latest all singin', all dancin' trainers. And if you find a pair that you like, and aren't all that bothered about changing fashions, then why not invest in two pairs?

Equipment

The home fitness equipment market is booming. There's a proliferation of manufacturers and retailers and an ever-expanding range of quality equipment. But one of the joys of Anyone, Anywhere, Anytime is that you need very little equipment. Just a sturdy chair or bench or the edge of a firm sofa; a step (the bottom step of a staircase will do), some light to medium weights (bottles of water are inexpensive and ideal for the job) and a well-padded mat or a few towels to lie on.

Getting
STARTED

Just the fact that you have bought this book indicates that you are serious about making some changes for the better where your health and fitness are concerned. But before you follow any of my Triple A workout programmes, you should first take some time to assess your present level of physical condition. The assessment that follows is not like a car's MOT test, where you pass or fail. Instead, you should view it as a way of establishing your overall fitness and providing you with a 'benchmark'. Your overall result will help you decide which of the fitness programmes you should start with. You can record the results of each of your tests on the page, or on a photocopy if you prefer to keep your book like new.

Questionnaire

Before you begin the fitness tests, invest a few minutes in completing my questionnaire. Be sure to answer all the questions and be honest with yourself. Circle or tick the statement you think best describes you. The numbers in brackets indicate your score for each question. Add your scores up when you've finished. As you progress with the Triple A exercise programme, you will want to test yourself from time to time to see how you are doing and you should repeat the questionnaire as well, since some of your answers should have changed since you first did it. Here goes for the first time!

1 AGE (which age category do you fall into?)

- Below 20 (score 3)
- 21–30 (score 2)
- 31–40 (score 1)
- 41 and over (score 0)

2 CARDIOVASCULAR HEALTH (the health of your heart and respiratory system)

- I have no history of heart or lung disease, nor does my immediate family (score 3)
- I have had successful treatment in the past and the doctor has given me the all clear (score 2)
- I have a problem, but am no longer receiving treatment (score 1)
- I am currently under medical supervision (score 0)

3 GENETICS (your family history)

- Both of my parents are still alive (score 3)
- One of my parents is still alive (score 2)
- Both of my parents lived long lives and have now passed away (score 1)
- Both of my parents died of natural causes before they were 60 years of age (score 0)

4 INJURIES (the condition of your muscles and joints)

- I am currently injury-free (score 3)
- I have recovered from an old injury and have had no recurrence (score 2)
- I am recovering from a recent injury (score 1)
- I am suffering from a painful injury at present (score 0)

5 ILLNESS (your overall health)

- I am in good general health, with no signs of illness (score 3)
- I am suffering mildly from ill health, but I'm recovering (score 2)
- I am particularly limited by illness (score 1)
- I am unable to do much without feeling the effect of my illness (score 0)

6 WEIGHT
(weigh yourself using accurate scales, then using the weight chart on page 46, find your ideal weight)

- I am within one kilo of my ideal weight **(score 3)**
- I am within 4 kilos of my ideal weight **(score 2)**
- I am 5–9 kilos above or below my ideal weight **(score 1)**
- I am 10 kilos or more above or below my ideal weight **(score 0)**

7 LIFESTYLE
(how much do you smoke?)

- I do not smoke and never have **(score 3)**
- I used to smoke but have now quit **(score 2)**
- I am a social, occasional smoker **(score 1)**
- I smoke regularly and have done for more than a year **(score 0)**

8 FOOD
(daily healthy food intake should consist of 3 balanced meals that include fresh produce, lean meat, poultry, fish, complex carbohydrate and water)

- I eat 3 regular, healthy balanced meals each day **(score 3)**
- I skip the odd meal here and there, eat only a few pieces of fresh produce and have a limited water intake **(score 2)**
- I eat lunch and an evening meal only, and do not always make sensible choices **(score 1)**
- I am very erratic, eating mainly ready-made meals with no fresh produce, and washed down with beer **(score 0)**

9 ALCOHOL
(how much do you drink?)

- I am teetotal **(score 3)**
- I drink less than 10 Units weekly **(score 2)**
- I drink no more than 14 (women) / 21 (men) Units weekly **(score 1)**
- I consume in excess of 18 (women) / 25 (men) Units weekly **(score 0)**

10 EXERCISE
(your level of physical activity)

- I am presently exercising fairly briskly 3 or more times a week **(score 3)**
- I am physically active, walking the dog and doing household chores on most days **(score 2)**
- I exercise occasionally, participating in the odd game of sport or going for a walk **(score 1)**
- I lead a totally sedentary lifestyle with no exercise whatsoever **(score 0)**

NOTE YOUR QUESTIONNAIRE SCORES HERE:

Date/score .... Date/score ....
Date/score .... Date/score ....
Date/score .... Date/score ....
Date/score .... Date/score ....
Date/score .... Date/score ....

Are you the size you should be?

Your body shape and weight impact on your overall wellbeing, so get out your bathroom scales and weigh yourself, then follow up by measuring your body dimensions and calculate your BMI. Make a note each time you measure up.

Ideal weight

The chart below shows your ideal weight range, depending on whether you have a small, medium or large frame. To use it, measure your height when you are not wearing any shoes, and weigh yourself without clothes. Use the chart in conjunction with the questionnaire on pages 44–45, and again, when you have been following the Triple A programme for 2–3 months, to follow your progress. Hopefully you'll be getting nearer to your goal all the time.

MAKE A NOTE OF YOUR BODY WEIGHT MEASUREMENTS HERE:

Date/weight ....   Date/weight ....
Date/weight ....   Date/weight ....
Date/weight ....   Date/weight ....
Date/weight ....   Date/weight ....
Date/weight ....   Date/weight ....
Date/weight ....   Date/weight ....
Date/weight ....   Date/weight ....
Date/weight ....   Date/weight ....
Date/weight ....   Date/weight ....

IDEAL HEIGHT(M)/WEIGHT(KG) FOR MEN			
Weight without clothes/Height without shoes			
Height	Small frame	Medium frame	Large frame
1.62	53.5–57.5	56.5–62	60–67.5
1.65	55–58.5	57.5–63	61.5–68.5
1.68	56.5–60.5	59–65	62.5–71
1.70	58–62.5	61–67	64.5–73
1.72	60–64	62.5–69	67–75.5
1.75	62–66	64.5–71	68.5–77
1.78	63.5–68	66.5–72.5	70.5–79
1.80	66.5–70	68–75	72.5–81.5
1.83	67.5–72	70–77.5	74.5–83.5
1.85	69–73.5	72–79.5	76.5–86
1.88	71–76	73.5–82	78–88
1.90	72.5–77.5	76–84	81–90.5
1.93	74.5–79.5	78–86.5	82.5–91.5

IDEAL HEIGHT(M)/WEIGHT(KG) FOR WOMEN			
Weight without clothes/Height without shoes			
Height	Small frame	Medium frame	Large frame
1.52	43.5–47	46–51.5	49.5–57
1.55	45–48.5	47–52.5	51–58
1.57	46.5–50	48.5–54	52.5–59.5
1.60	47.5–51	50–55.5	53.5–61
1.62	49–52.5	51.5–57.5	55–62.5
1.65	50.5–54	52.5–59	57–64.5
1.68	52–55.5	54.5–61.5	58.5–66.5
1.70	53.5–57.5	56.5–63	60.5–68
1.72	55.5–59.5	58–65	62.5–70
1.75	57.5–61.5	60–66	66–72
1.78	59–63.5	62–68.5	68.5–74

Body dimensions

Get an idea of your general physique by measuring the girth of certain parts of your body. All you need is a tape measure and, preferably, someone to help. Be careful to apply the tape lightly but firmly, and relax – no moving the fat around under the tape or sucking in your tummy. Measure at the same spot every time.

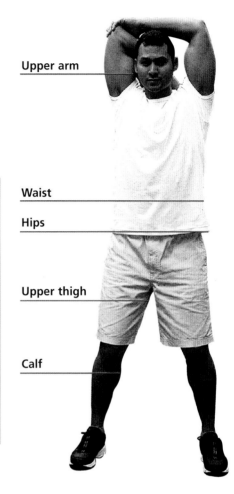

Upper arm

Waist

Hips

Upper thigh

Calf

MAKE A NOTE OF YOUR BODY DIMENSIONS HERE:

Upper arm (left)	**Upper thigh (left)**
Date/measurement...................	Date/measurement...................
Date/measurement	Date/measurement ....
Upper arm (right)	**Upper thigh (right)**
Date/measurement...................	Date/measurement...................
Date/measurement	Date/measurement ....
Waist	**Calf (left)**
Date/measurement...................	Date/measurement...................
Date/measurement	Date/measurement ....
Hips	**Calf (right)**
Date/measurement...................	Date/measurement...................
Date/measurement	Date/measurement ....

Body mass index test (BMI)

Body mass index test (BMI)

The most accurate method of determining the correct weight for your height is to calculate your Body Mass Index. The recommended BMI for men is set between 21 and 26, while for women it is 18–23. It is arrived at by dividing your body weight in kilograms by your height in metres squared.

FOR EXAMPLE, for a man of 1.75 metres weighing 78.75 kilos, the calculation is as follows:
Height squared: 1.75m x 1.75m = **3.06m**
78.75 kilos divided by **3.06 metres = BMI of 25.73**
Now calculate your own BMI and make a note of the result.

RECORD YOUR BMI READINGS HERE:

Date/index	Date/index ....
Date/index	Date/index ....

HOW WELL DID I DO?

Men	21–26 = **normal** (score 3)
	27–30 = **below normal** (score 2)
	31–35 = **poor** (score 1)
	36–40 = **very poor** (score 0)
Women	18–23 = **normal** (score 3)
	24–27 = **below normal** (score 2)
	28–32 = **poor** (score 1)
	33–37 = **very poor** (score 0)

Simple fitness testing

Now you've completed the questionnaire, made a note of your body dimensions and checked your BMI, you're ready to take the simple fitness tests. These, together with the results of the questionnaire, will not only help you evaluate your current level of fitness, but will also enable you to decide which of my Triple A programmes is most suited to you – the Exercise Newcomer, the Exercise Restarter, the Regular Exerciser or the Vigorous Exerciser. You shouldn't find the fitness tests too difficult or time-consuming. On the contrary, you will probably enjoy the challenge, and the results will tell you a lot about your physical condition.

The tests will also be useful to you later on, when regular exercise has become a part of your normal lifestyle. And although you will certainly feel better as a result of following the Triple A programme, the physical changes are often hard to recognise because they occur gradually. That's why I recommend that you retest yourself every 2–3 months. Not only will it reveal your progress, but it will add to your confidence that you are improving your overall condition. As your results and scores improve, you will enjoy a greater sense of accomplishment and satisfaction, and as we all know, there's nothing like success to keep up the motivation levels.

If you experience any discomfort, dizziness or nausea when you're doing any of the exercises, then stop and consult your doctor.

Don't forget to record your values for each test.

Testing for excess fat

A I have a flat stomach coupled with no 'love handles'

B I can pinch more than 2.5cm, but less than 5cm on any part of my waistline

C I can grab more than a handful of soft flesh from my 'love handles'

D From a standing position, I can't see my toes without bending forwards

HOW WELL DID I DO?
A Keep up the good work. **(score 3)**
B You're not doing too badly, but keep a watchful eye open. **(score 2)**
C Deal with those 'love handles' before they get out of control. **(score 1)**
D Your body's in a bad state and you need to get it back on track. **(score 0)**

Testing for cardiovascular fitness

Check your resting heart rate

Before you begin this test, ensure that you have become proficient at checking your pulse rate manually (see pages 36–37). Sit down in a comfortable armchair. Avoid any exciting or stressful distractions, whether environmental or emotional. Wait a few minutes, then measure your resting heart rate. You may wish to try a few times over a 10-minute period. If you end up with varying readings, take an average of your findings.

NOTE YOUR RESTING HEART RATE (RHR) READINGS HERE:

Date/RHR ....

Date/RHR ....

Date/RHR ....

Date/RHR ....

HOW WELL DID I DO?

60 BPM or below = **excellent** (score 4)

61–70 BPM = **good** (score 3)

71–75 BPM = **average** (score 2)

76–80 BPM = **below average** (score 1)

81 and below = **poor** (score 0)   *(BPM = Beats per minute)*

The step test

There's no need to buy a step for this. It can be done on a staircase. Be sure that you prepare your body by doing a few warm-up exercises first (see pages 56–59).

1 Find a platform or step. It should be between 30cm and 40cm high.

2 Keep your back straight and stomach muscles tucked in.

3 As you do the test, swing your arms naturally as if you are walking.

4 Step up on the platform with your entire foot. Be careful not under- or over-step the platform.

5 Start stepping up and down at a non-stop, steady pace for 3 minutes (right foot up, left foot up, right foot down, left foot down).

6 Breathe normally and continuously throughout the test.

7 Stop, then immediately sit down and start taking your recovery heart rate for 6 seconds, multiplying by 10 to calculate for one whole minute.

NOTE YOUR RECOVERY HEART RATE (RHR) READINGS HERE:

Date/RHR ....

Date/RHR ....

Date/RHR ....

Date/RHR ....

Date/RHR ....

Date/RHR ....

Date/RHR ....

Date/RHR ....

Date/RHR ....

Date/RHR ....

HOW WELL DID I DO?

75 or below = **excellent** (score 3)

76–85 = **good** (score 2)

86–100 = **average** (score 1)

101 or above = **poor** (score 0)

These scores apply to men or women

Muscular strength and endurance testing

This component of your personal fitness test aims to identify the overall state of your strength and endurance by using three key exercises. You'll be using the Press Up – this tests the general condition of your upper body; the Basic Curl Up – for checking out the condition of your mid-section – and finally, to test for lower body strength, you'll do the Static Squat Test. These tests can often induce a competitive spirit in even the most hardened exercise refuser. But it's not a contest, so take my advice and work at a pace that's both comfortable and safe. It's vitally important to maintain good form and technique and to breathe correctly throughout. You should breathe out on exertion and in on the return of each exercise. When you can no longer continue to exercise comfortably, the test is at an end.

Finally, you should be adequately warmed up from having done the Step Test (see page 49). If for any reason you feel that your body has cooled down, then do some of the simple warm up exercises and stretches on pages 56–63.

And now let's start. Good luck!

Modified press up test

1 Kneel on all fours on the floor on a mat or other padded surface, distributing your body weight evenly over your hands and knees. Make sure your hands are flat on the floor and just wider than shoulder-width apart.

2 Take your weight slightly forwards so your shoulders are directly over your hands, then raise your feet off the floor.

3 Bend your elbows to lower your chest to the floor.

4 Extend your arms to return. Repeat as many times as you can.

RECORD YOUR RESULTS HERE:
Date/number...................................
Date/number...............................
HOW WELL DID I DO?
51 or more = **excellent** (score 3)
31–50 = **good** (score 2)
16–30 = **average** (score 1)
15 or below = **poor** (score 0)

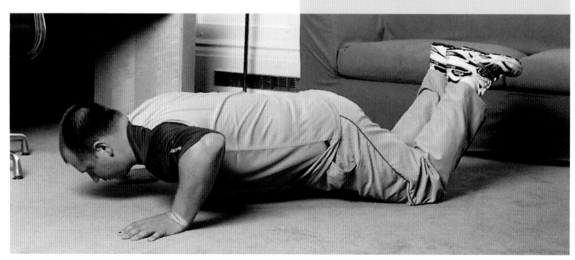

Basic curl up test

1 Lying on your back, raise both legs to a right angle, place your hands behind your ears to support your head, then raise your head, leaving a gap between chin and chest.

2 Draw in your tummy muscles and exhale as you curl your head and shoulders off the ground, bringing your elbows towards your knees.

3 To complete, inhale as you lower your body to position 1. Repeat as many times as you can.

RECORD YOUR RESULTS HERE:

Date/number...............................

Date/number...............................

Date/number...............................

Date/number...............................

HOW WELL DID I DO?

51 or more = **excellent** (score 3)

31–50 = **good** (score 2)

16–30 = **average** (score 1)

15 or below = **poor** (score 0)

Static squat test

1 Stand with your back flat against a firm surface and your feet about a hip-width apart.

2 Inhale as you bend your knees until your body forms a right angle. Keep your breathing regular throughout.

3 Hold for as long as comfortable using a watch to time yourself.

RECORD YOUR RESULTS HERE:

Date/seconds...........................

Date/seconds...........................

Date/seconds...........................

Date/seconds...........................

HOW WELL DID I DO?

61 seconds and above = **excellent** (score 3)

41–60 seconds = **good** (score 2)

31–40 seconds = **average** (score 1)

0–30 seconds = **poor** (score 0)

NOW ADD UP YOUR TOTAL SCORES – INCLUDING THE QUESTIONNAIRE – TO SEE HOW YOU DID

Total Score

IF YOU SCORED THE MAXIMUM OF 52 POINTS, then your rating is high and your suitability for exercising gets the green light. You may wish to choose the Vigorous Exerciser programme.

IF YOU SCORED MORE THAN 35, then your rating is good and you'll probably progress quite rapidly with the Regular Exerciser programme.

A SCORE OF BETWEEN 15 AND 34 suggests you should be taking stock of your current physical condition. Start by following either the Exercise Newcomer or the Exercise Restarter programme.

IF YOUR SCORE IS BELOW 15, you may be at risk if you do any of the exercise programmes. Ask your doctor's advice before you start.

THE
exercise
PROGRAMMES

Now you've reached the four exercise programmes. Each starts with a warm up and finishes with a cool down, and each is divided into two – an aerobic programme and a toning programme. All four are effective, easy to follow and clearly show the best way to incorporate aerobic activity and overall body toning in your exercise plan. And not only are they great for fat and inch loss, but also for a healthy heart and lungs and increased bone density. If you don't want to do the toning programme straight after the aerobic exercise but wish to do them on different days, that's fine, but you must include your warm up before you start toning.

Before and after you exercise

Your body isn't ready for work until it's warmed up and stretched. Even simple exercises will seem hard and you risk injury. And a cool down and stretch is the best way to end your session. The exercises are the same for both. Mix and match them for variety, but whatever you do, don't forget to do them. They don't take long.

Warming up

Our bodies are more efficient when they are warm, and less likely to suffer damage. So, it is vital to warm up as a prelude to more vigorous exercise. If you're in a cold environment, wear warm, loose clothing.

WARMING UP

• Prepares the body for exercise by increasing circulation and delivering more oxygen to the muscles.
• Raises body temperature so the body is more efficient and less likely to suffer damage during exercise.
• Increases the heart rate in readiness for more strenuous exercise.
• Mobilises the joints so they move more freely and are less likely to be damaged.

For the best and safest results you should begin any of the exercise programmes with 5–10 minutes of warm ups (see pages 56–59). You can either work through my suggestions in order, or pick and choose to add variety. As you do the warm ups, gradually increase the pace and intensity to raise your heart rate to your aerobic training zone (see pages 36–37). And finally, add some stretching exercises from those I offer (see opposite and pages 60–63).

Cooling down

The cool down lowers the intensity of the exercise. It's the part a lot of people forget, but in fact, it's more important to cool down than it is to warm up. If you don't, you can suffer from light-headedness, fainting, or even – the worst-case scenario – death.

What happens is this. When you're engaged in fairly intensive exercise, particularly exercise sustained for a relatively long period, the heart pumps blood at an increased rate to the entire body, especially to the working muscles. If you suddenly stop exercising, there's a rapid decline of the heart rate and the heart stops pumping blood around the whole body. The blood can then pool in the trunk, instead of returning to the heart, and this can be fatal. But if you do your cool downs after you exercise, the movement of your limbs massages the veins and helps the blood back to the heart.

As with warm ups, you should follow your cooling down session with some stretches (see opposite and pages 60–63).

COOLING DOWN

• Eliminates waste from the muscles.
• Reduces soreness and injury.
• Replenishes fuel supplies in the muscles.
• Increases suppleness.

Stretching

Warming up and cooling down should both be followed by some stretching exercises. Although there is much debate as to the usefulness of stretching before you exercise, I personally believe that it is valuable, especially for the major working muscles. Stretching also helps to 'fire up' your muscle receptors and acts a catalyst in preparing the body as a whole. And when it comes to cooling down, the stretches should never be omitted.

How many and how much

Firstly, you need to understand that a 'repetition' (or 'rep') is one complete, single exercise. A 'circuit' or 'set' is a complete series or set of exercises.

Start by looking at the pictures and studying each exercise. You may decide to give each one a 'dummy run', in which case, be sure to warm up first. Once you are confident, it's time for the 'real thing' – the sets and reps. The tempo of each exercise is as crucial as good form, so work at a steady and controlled pace.

Avoid rushing your circuit and if an exercise becomes difficult to complete, then pause for a short time. It's better not to sacrifice good form, than to continue and cause injury as this will ultimately lead to setbacks in your crusade for a better body.

The chart suggests the number of circuits, e.g. 2, followed by the number of repetitions you should perform, e.g. 10, in each workout. The chart below indicates what you should be aiming for in each of the given workouts. It illustrates how to progress over the forthcoming weeks.

	Week 1	Week 2	Week 3	Week 4	Week 5	Week 6	Week 7
The Newcomer Programme	2 x 10 (2 circuits with 10 reps for each exercise)	2 x 12	2 x 14	2 x 16	3 x 10	3 x 12	Move on to the Restarter programme.
The Restarter Programme	2 x 10	2 x 12	2 x 14	2 x 16	3 x 10	3 x 12	Add 2 extra reps per week until you have completed 20 reps. Then move on to the Regular programme.
The Regular Programme	3 x 12	3 x 14	3 x 16	3 x 18	3 x 20	3 x 22.	Add 2 extra reps per week until you have completed 26 reps. Then move on to the Vigorous programme.
The Vigorous Programme	3 x 12	3 x 14	3 x 16	3 x 18	4 x 14	4 x 16	For continued progress, add more reps and circuits or try doing the exercises in a different order. Also try timed circuits, i.e. performing each exercise for 1 minute for a certain number of circuits.

WARM UPS & COOL DOWNS

1 Skipping or jump roping

Start with the rope behind you. As you swing the rope forwards over your head, rotate your wrist, not your shoulders (a common mistake) and jump slightly off the ground so the rope swings freely under your feet. Start slowly and build up speed when you can. For a warm up, continue for 3–5 minutes, trying sets of 15–20 jumps with a small pause in between, otherwise you'll be breathless even before you start your main exercise programme!

2 On the spot jogging

The pure simplicity of this exercise and the fact that it requires no equipment allows you to perform it anywhere. Just jog or bounce lightly from one leg to the other so that one foot is always in contact with the ground. Land softly, ensuring the heel of the landing foot presses down. Swing the arms across the body as you jog on the spot.

3 Step up

Find a suitable platform or step – one that ensures your knees do not bend at more than a right angle. If you are following the Newcomer or Restarter programmes, you'll need a lower platform. Step on and off the platform at a slow to moderate pace, making sure your foot is placed securely on the platform to help you keep your balance. You can either alternate legs with each step or perform a predetermined number with one leg then change legs.

4 Across the body punch

Stand with your feet wide apart, making a loose fist with each hand. Bend your knees into a gentle squat, move your torso to the left and punch lightly out and across your body to the left with your right arm, simultaneously lifting your right heel off the ground. Then immediately swing your torso to the right and use your left arm to punch out and across to the right, lifting your left heel. Build up to a good pace.

WARM UPS & COOL DOWNS

5

In motion overhead press

Stand with your feet wide apart and raise your arms to shoulder-level. Perform a light squat as you move your torso over to one side, at the same time pressing your arms above your head. As you go back to the centre, return your arms to shoulder level. Move immediately to the opposite side, again pressing your arms above your head.

6

Knee up with chest press

Hold your arms at chest level, palms facing outwards, then raise each knee in turn. With each movement, push your arms away from your chest, then immediately return them to the start position. Avoid any heavy stamping of your feet.

Knee up with arm curl

Make a loose fist with each hand, tuck your elbows into your sides, then raise each knee in turn. With each movement, curl your hands up towards your shoulders. Avoid any heavy stamping down of your feet.

Heel up with criss-cross arm

Start by pushing off lightly from one foot to the other, bringing your heels up to your buttocks and keeping your arms at chest height, elbows bent. Gradually start pushing your elbows outwards as you jump. As you bring your arms back to your body, take one arm under the other, alternating arms as you go, left arm over right arm, right over left, etc.

STRETCHES

Shoulder stretch

Stand with your feet slightly apart, tummy muscles tight and knees slightly bent. Rotating your wrists, raise your arms above your head and place your palms together. Now straighten your arms as much as you can until you feel a stretch in your shoulders. Breathe continuously throughout. Hold for 15–30 seconds.

Upper arm stretch

Stand with your feet slightly apart, tummy tight and knees slightly bent. Raise one arm, then lower it so the hand of that arm lies between your shoulder blades. Now place your free hand on the elbow of the arm being stretched. Gently ease the elbow behind your head until you feel a positive stretch. Keep your breathing regular throughout and hold for 15–30 seconds. Change sides and repeat.

Outer shoulder stretch

Stand with your feet slightly apart, tummy tight and knees slightly bent. Place one arm across your chest and cup the hand of your free arm over the elbow of the first arm. Apply gentle pressure to the elbow with your hand until you feel a positive, pain-free stretch in your outer shoulder. Keep your breathing regular throughout and hold the stretch for 15–30 seconds. Change sides and repeat.

Chest stretch

Stand with your feet slightly apart, tummy tight and knees slightly bent. Take both hands behind your back, link your fingers and turn your palms in. Gently raise your arms away from your body, simultaneously bringing your shoulder blades together until you feel a positive stretch in your chest. Keep your breathing regular throughout and hold the stretch for 15–30 seconds.

STRETCHES

5

Back stretch

Stand with your feet slightly apart, tummy tight and knees slightly bent. Place your arms in front of you, linking your fingers together and with your palms turned in towards you. Bring your tummy in and curve your entire back outwards. Gently push your arms forwards and away from your body until you feel a positive stretch in your back. Keep your breathing regular throughout and hold the stretch for 15–30 seconds.

6

Rear thigh (hamstring) stretch

Place one foot in front of the other and slightly raise the front foot. Slightly bend your rear leg. Place your hands on your thighs and lean gently forwards until you feel a positive stretch along the length of the rear thigh muscle of the front leg. Keep your breathing regular throughout and hold the stretch for 15–30 seconds. Change to the other leg and repeat.

Front thigh (quadricep) stretch

To support yourself, hold on to a steady surface. Slightly bend one leg, then raise the other leg up behind you and grasp your ankle, gently bringing your heel towards your buttock. Push your hips gently forwards and ease the leg backwards until you feel a positive stretch in the front thigh. Keep your breathing regular throughout and hold this stretch for 15–30 seconds. Change to the other leg and repeat.

Lower leg (calf) stretch

Brace yourself against a solid, steady support. Step one leg forwards and bend that knee slightly. Keep the rear leg fairly straight. Lean forwards and/or place your legs further apart to increase the degree of stretch in the lower back leg. Keep your breathing regular throughout and hold this stretch for 15–30 seconds. Change to the other leg and repeat.

Newcomer
AEROBIC CIRCUIT

Treat my Newcomer programme as your introduction to exercise and when you are following it, remember your magic number three. That's because, to see a steady improvement in your overall fitness, you need to do the programme three times a week. Don't give up after a few days though and say it isn't working. You need to continue for at least six weeks to see results.

NEWCOMER AEROBIC CIRCUIT

1 Marching on the spot

March on the spot, raising your knees up to hip level. Swing your opposite arm with your opposite leg in a marching fashion. Avoid heavy stamping of the feet and keep your breathing regular throughout. Maintain for 30 seconds.

2 Press up against a wall

Stand about 70cm away from a wall, feet slightly apart. Place the palms of your hands against the wall, slightly wider than shoulder-width apart, but at the same level. Inhale as you bend your elbows to a right angle. Exhale as you return, extending your arms without locking them. Keep your tummy muscles tight and your back straight throughout. Continue for the desired number of repetitions.

3
Abdominal curl

Lying on your back, bend your knees and place your hands behind your ears to support your head. Maintain a tennis-ball size gap between your chin and your chest. Draw in your tummy muscles and exhale as you raise your head and shoulders off the ground. Inhale as you lower your head and shoulders to return. Continue for the desired number of repetitions.

4
Leg squat

With your feet turned slightly outwards and a little wider than a hip-width apart, fold your arms and hold them in front of you at chest height. Inhale as you bend your knees no lower than a right angle. As you bend, your upper body will tilt forwards. Maintain a straight back and look directly ahead throughout. To return, exhale as you straighten your legs, avoiding full extension. Continue for the desired number of repetitions.

NEWCOMER AEROBIC CIRCUIT

Floor arm dip

Sit on the ground with your feet flat and slightly apart and your knees bent. The palms of your hands should be slightly turned in and roughly a hip-width apart. Keeping the knees bent, draw in your tummy muscles and raise your hips off the ground. Inhale as you bend at the elbows to lower your buttocks towards the ground, but without resting them there. To return, exhale as you extend your arms. Avoid 'locking out' of the elbows and forceful thrusting of the hips. Continue for the desired number of repetitions.

5

Abdominal curl up 6

Lying on your back, raise both legs to a right angle, place your hands behind your ears to support your head, then raise your head, leaving a gap between chin and chest. Draw in your tummy muscles and exhale as you curl your head and shoulders off the ground, bringing your elbows towards your knees. To complete, inhale as you lower your body to the start position. Continue for the desired number of repetitions.

Calf raise 7

Standing with your hands on your hips for balance, place your feet about 15cm apart. Look directly ahead and maintain a straight back by keeping your tummy muscles tight. Raise your heels from the ground until you are on the balls of your feet, then exhale. To return, inhale then lower your feet to the ground. Continue for the desired number of repetitions.

NEWCOMER AEROBIC CIRCUIT

8 Marching elbow to knee

Stand with your feet together then bring your arms to shoulder level and bend your elbows to form a right angle. March on the spot, raising your knees as you go and twisting slightly from side to side to bring one elbow to the opposite knee. Draw in your tummy muscles, keep your breathing regular throughout and avoid heavy stamping of the feet and excessive twisting of the body. Continue for the desired number of repetitions.

9 Box press up

Kneel on all fours with your hands slightly more than shoulder-width apart and knees directly under your hips to form a 'box' shape with your body. Inhale as you bend your elbows outwards to lower your chest towards the ground, keeping your head up slightly and with a straight, flat back throughout. Do not force your elbows. To return, exhale as you gradually extend your arms without locking them. Continue for the desired number of repetitions.

Abdominal reverse curl 10

Lying on your back, raise both legs to a right angle. Keeping your head back, and your feet together, place your hands under your head, then gently draw in your tummy muscles and exhale as you raise your knees slightly towards your chest. Your buttocks and hips will come slightly off the ground at the same time. Inhale as you return your knees to the start position. Continue for the desired number of repetitions.

Alternate partial lunge with arm curl 11

Stand with your arms at your sides and make a light fist with your hands. Step forwards at least 75cm with one foot, bending the knee slightly. As you step, inhale and curl both arms up. To return, exhale as you push backwards, slightly straightening the front leg and extending your arms. Repeat, starting with the other leg. Continue for the desired number of repetitions.

QUICK FIX PROGRAMME: When you're pressed for time and can only manage the bare minimum, I suggest you do a set of 10–12 reps of exercises 3, 4, 9 and 10.

Newcomer

TONING PROGRAMME

These exercises have been designed to target the most
stubborn and troublesome areas of the body. If you do
them regularly, they will lead to a flatter stomach, a more
toned body and better looking legs. You should aim to
complete one set of 12–15 reps of each exercise at
every session. Make sure you perform them slowly and in
a well-controlled manner.

Single arm–knee reach

Works the abdominals

Lying on your back, bend both knees and place your right hand on your right thigh. Maintaining a gap between chin and chest, exhale as you curl your shoulders off the ground and slide your hand up your thigh towards your knee. To finish, inhale as you return. Continue for the desired number of repetitions, then change sides.

Cross-over curl

Works the abdominals and obliques

Lying on your back, place your hands behind your ears for support and bend your knees. Cross one leg over the other. Exhale as you curl up with a slight twisting action so the opposite elbow travels towards the raised knee. To finish, inhale as you return. Continue for the desired number of repetitions, then change sides.

3

Single leg squat off step

Works thighs and buttocks

Stand parallel to a step no higher than 40cm and place the foot nearest the step on it. With hands on hips for balance and a straight back, inhale as you bend the leg on the step and exhale as you straighten it. As you do this, the foot on the floor will come off the ground slightly. Avoid bouncing. Continue for the desired number of repetitions, then repeat with the other leg.

4

Standing side leg lift

Works outer thigh and hip

Hold onto a support with one hand, placing your free hand on your waist for balance. Soften the knee of the supporting leg and flex the foot of the other leg. Exhale as you raise the working leg 45–50cm from the ground. Inhale as you lower the leg. Take care not to raise the leg excessively as this will result in a tilted body. Continue for the desired number of repetitions, then change sides.

5

Standing rear leg lift

Works the buttocks

Hold onto a support with one hand, placing your free hand on your waist for balance. Soften the knee of the supporting leg, tilt your upper body fractionally forwards and flex the foot of the working leg. Exhale as you squeeze your buttock muscles momentarily and lift the working leg behind you. Inhale as you return. Continue for the desired number of repetitions, then change sides.

6

Standing adductor squeeze

Works the inner thigh

Hold onto a support with one hand, placing your free hand on your waist for balance. Soften the knee of the supporting leg and flex and turn out the foot of the working leg. Exhale as you briefly squeeze your inner thigh muscles and move the working leg across the other. Inhale as you return. Continue for the desired number of repetitions, then change sides.

Remember to cool down and stretch (see pages 56–63).

Restarter
AEROBIC CIRCUIT

At Restarter level you'll still be working out three times a week if you want to achieve ongoing improvement, but now the intensity of your training is stepped up. In addition, you'll start to target some parts of your body with more than one exercise and you'll also be increasing your number of reps and circuits.

RESTARTER AEROBIC CIRCUIT

1 Jumping jack

Start with your feet close together and your arms at your sides. Exhale as you gently jump your feet apart, raising your arms as shown. Soften your knees as you land gently with your feet flat on the ground. Inhale as you jump your feet gently in to return. Continue for the desired number of repetitions.

2 Leg lunge

Stand with your hands on your waist. Inhale as you step forwards at least 75cm with one foot, bending the knee to no more than a right angle. The rear leg will naturally bend to the same degree. Ensure that the toes of both feet are pointing forwards. To return, exhale as you push backwards with the front leg until you are in the neutral start position. Continue for the desired number of repetitions, then change sides.

Chair/bench arm dip

Stand with your back to a solid support and place your hands over the edge of the support, roughly a hip-width apart. Take your feet slightly forwards, distributing your body weight evenly over your hands and feet. Keeping your hips low and knees bent, look directly ahead. Inhale, keeping your elbows partially tucked in as you bend your elbows to a right angle. To complete the movement, exhale as you semi-extend the elbows. Continue for the desired number of repetitions.

3

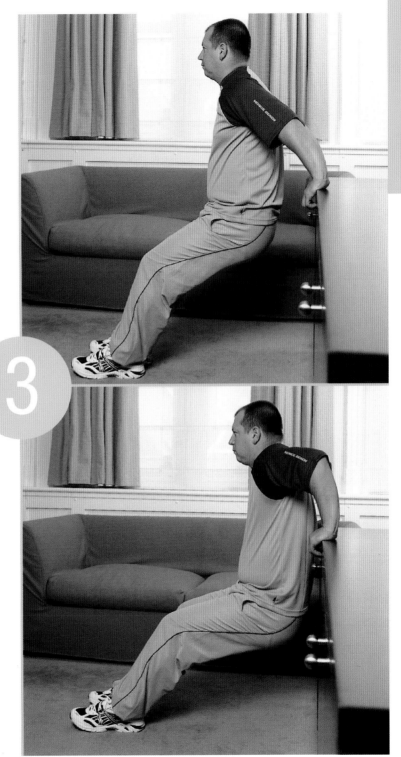

RESTARTER AEROBIC CIRCUIT

4 Bicycle abs

Lying on your back, place your hands behind your ears for support, lift your head and shoulders, raise both legs and bend the knees to 90 degrees. Keeping your head and shoulders lifted, twist your upper body so your left elbow meets your right knee while your left leg semi-extends. Then twist to the other side, bringing your right elbow to your left knee. Continue to alternate, keeping your breathing regular throughout, for the desired number of repetitions.

5 Spotty dog

Stand with your left arm forwards and your left leg back, then do a gentle jump while taking your right arm forwards and your right leg back. Keep your torso slightly tilted and your breathing regular throughout. Continue to alternate for the desired number of repetitions.

Front leg kick 6

With your right leg back, adopt an 'on guard' stance, raising your arms and making a fist as if to protect your face and torso. Breathing out, bring your right leg forwards, kicking gently out to the front and avoiding flexing the right knee. Inhale as you bring your right leg back to the start position. Continue for the desired number of repetitions, then change legs.

Lying toe reach 7

Lying on your back, raise and keep your legs semi-extended. Keeping a small gap between chin and chest, exhale as you extend your arms above and over your body, curling your torso and stretching until your fingertips almost meet your toes. Inhale as you lower your body to the start position. Continue for the desired number of repetitions.

RESTARTER AEROBIC CIRCUIT

8 Plié squat

Stand with your feet turned slightly outwards a little more than a hip-width apart. Point your hands downwards between your legs, then inhale as you bend at your knees, no lower than to a right angle. As you bend, your upper body will tilt slightly forwards. Keep a straight back and look directly ahead throughout. To return, exhale as you straighten your legs, avoiding full extension. Continue for the desired number of repetitions.

9 Assisted press up

Stand facing a solid support, extend your arms and place your hands over the edge of the support, slightly more than shoulder-width apart. Take your feet a hip-width apart and look slightly upwards. Keeping a straight back, inhale as you bend your elbows to lower your chest to the support. Exhale as you semi-extend your elbows to return to the start position. Continue for the desired number of repetitions.

Knee reach 10

Lying on the ground, bend both knees up, keeping your feet together. Place your hands on your thighs and maintaining a small gap between chin and chest, exhale as you draw in your tummy muscles and curl your head and shoulders up, sliding your hands up your thighs towards your knees. To return, inhale as you lower your head and shoulders. Continue for the desired number of repetitions.

Alternate side leg lunge 11

Stand with your legs wide and your feet pointing outwards. Place your hands on your hips and lunge sideways, taking your weight from one leg to the other. Each pair of movements counts as one complete repetition. Continue for the desired number of repetitions, breathing naturally throughout.

QUICK FIX PROGRAMME: Too busy or too tired to go the whole hog today? You'll feel more energised if you give exercises 2, 3, 4, 7 and 10 a go. Do one set of 12–15 reps each.

Restarter

TONING PROGRAMME

A more defined and shapelier body doesn't just appear miraculously overnight. It requires a combination of hard work and effective exercise. You'll find the exercises in this Restarter toning programme not only fun, but fast acting. They've been designed to give you maximum results in minimum time using minimum equipment. Aim to do one or two sets of 15–20 reps per exercise session and you'll soon notice the difference.

Narrow press up

Works rear upper arms, shoulders and inner chest

On all-fours, place your hands on the ground slightly less than shoulder-width apart. Raise your feet. Bring your weight over your hands, keeping your tummy muscles in and your head slightly up. Bend your elbows, keeping them tucked in. Inhale as you lower your chest, then exhale, extending your arms without locking them. Continue for the desired number of repetitions.

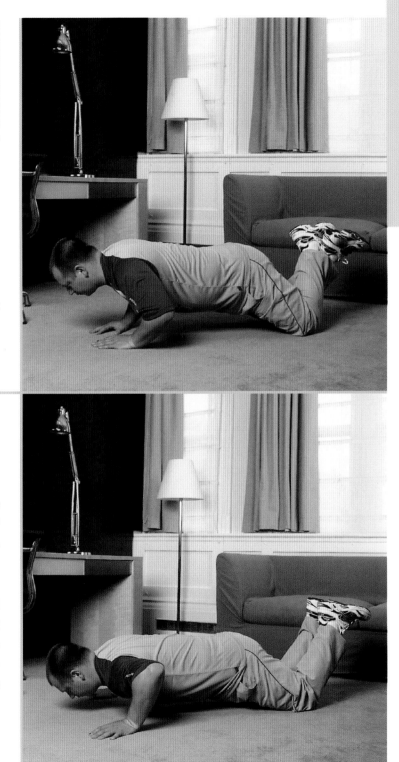

Wide press up

Works outer chest, shoulders and rear upper arms

Kneeling on all-fours, place your hands wider than shoulder-width apart. Bring your weight forwards over your hands. Keep your tummy muscles drawn in and your head slightly up. Inhale as you bend your elbows and lower your chest to the ground. To return, exhale as you semi-extend your arms. Continue for the desired number of repetitions.

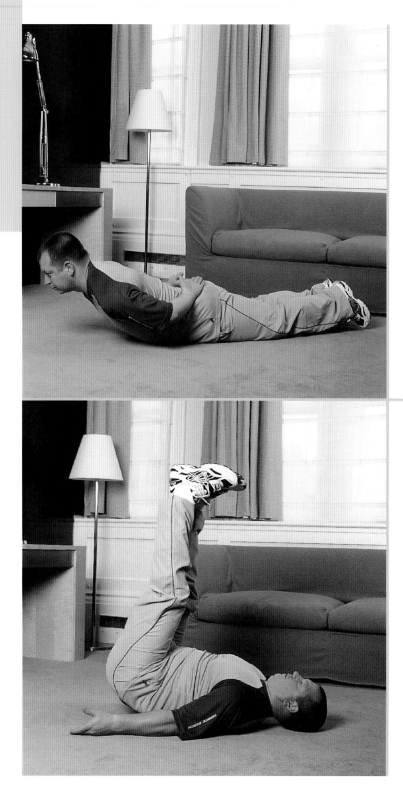

3
Lumbar extension

Works lower back

Face-down on the ground, place your hands on your lower back, palms upwards. Inhale as you raise your head, chest and shoulders no more than 15–20cm. Exhale, squeezing your buttocks together. To return, inhale as you relax the buttocks and lower your head, chest and shoulders to the ground. Keep your feet together and in contact with the ground throughout. Continue for the desired number of repetitions.

4
Vertical reverse curl

Works lower abdominals

Lying on the ground, place your hands at the sides of your body with the palms facing upwards. Exhale as you draw in your tummy muscles, then gently raise your legs until your hips are slightly off the ground. Keep your head back throughout. To return, inhale as you gently lower your legs and hips to the start position. Continue for the desired number of repetitions.

5

Glute squeeze

Works buttocks

Lying on your back with your arms at your sides and your feet flat and a little apart, bend your knees and raise your hips slightly off the ground. Exhaling and squeezing your buttock muscles together, raise your hips slightly higher. To return, inhale as you lower your hips to the start position. Keep your head back and your tummy muscles drawn in throughout. Continue for the desired number of repetitions.

6

Adductor shaper

Works inner thighs

Lying on your back, put your hands under your buttocks for support. With your head back, raise your legs, keeping your feet flexed towards you, knees slightly bent and tummy muscles drawn in. Exhale as you steadily open your legs outwards as far as comfortable. To return, inhale as you gradually bring your legs together. Continue for the desired number of repetitions.

Remember to cool down and stretch (see pages 56–63).

13

Regular
AEROBIC CIRCUIT

12

11

By now you will be experiencing the discipline of a regular routine and from here on in, your exercise will become even more varied, interesting and enjoyable. By sticking with it, progressing through your Regular programme and committing yourself, you will continue to see great improvements. But the key is to keep your exercise intensity high and your number of workouts frequent.

REGULAR AEROBIC CIRCUIT

Jogging twistee

1 Stand with your torso twisting slightly in the opposite direction to your lower body and your arms at shoulder-height. Perform a small jump, landing softly on your feet, and as you jump, partially rotate your torso and your lower body in the opposite direction. Keep your head facing forwards and your arms at shoulder-height throughout and breathe in and out continuously. Continue, alternating direction, for the desired number of repetitions.

Dumbbell overhead press

Stand upright with a straight back, holding a light weight in each hand at shoulder level. Place one leg in front of the other. Keeping your tummy muscles drawn in, exhale and extend your arms above your head until the weights almost meet.

Inhale as you return your arms to shoulder level. Continue for the desired number of repetitions.

REGULAR AEROBIC CIRCUIT

3 Mummy crunch

Lying on your back with your knees bent, cross your arms over your chest. Keeping a small gap between your chin and chest, draw in your tummy muscles and exhale as you curl your shoulders off the ground. Inhale as you lower your shoulders to the ground to return to the start position. Continue for the desired number of repetitions.

4 Lateral squat with arm raise

Stand with your feet about a hip-width apart. Take your weight onto one leg, squatting a little as you do so. At the same time, raise both arms to the sides of your body and lift your free leg off the ground behind you. Keep your breathing regular throughout. Continue for the desired number of repetitions, alternating sides.

Dumbbell bent over row

Stand with one foot slightly in front of the other, knees bent, holding a weight in each hand and with your upper body tilted slightly forwards. Maintaining a straight back and with your tummy muscles drawn in throughout, exhale as you gently pull the weights up, bending your elbows outwards as you do so. Keep your head facing forwards. To return, inhale as you lower the weights to the start position. Continue for the desired number of repetitions.

5

REGULAR AEROBIC CIRCUIT

6 Dumbbell single leg calf raise

Standing with a weight in one hand hold on to a support for balance if required and lift the opposite leg to the hand holding the weight. Cross the raised leg behind the standing one. As you exhale, come up on the ball of the standing foot. To return, inhale as you lower the foot completely to the ground. Continue for the desired number of repetitions, then change sides.

7 Alternate 'V' sit up

Lying on your back, bend your knees and raise your arms above your head. Exhale as you raise your head and shoulders off the ground, simultaneously elevating one leg and taking your fingertips up to meet the foot of the raised leg. Inhale as you lower your head, shoulders and leg to the start position. Continue for the desired number of repetitions, alternating legs with each repetition.

8

Dumbbell arm curl

With one foot slightly in front of the other hold a weight in each hand with your elbows tucked in to the sides of your body and your arms extended. Maintaining a straight back and with your tummy muscles drawn in throughout, exhale as you gently curl your arms up, keeping your elbows tucked in. Inhale as you lower your arms to return. Continue for the desired number of repetitions.

9

Dumbbell leg squat

Stand with your feet slightly wider than a hip-width apart. Hold a weight in each hand and place the weights on your shoulders. Inhale as you bend your knees until your legs are parallel to the ground. Exhale as you semi-extend your legs to the start position. Continue for the desired number of repetitions.

REGULAR AEROBIC CIRCUIT

10 Jogging knee-up

Jog gently on the spot holding your hands at waist height in front of you, palms down. As you jog, raise your knees so they touch your hands each time. Keep your breathing regular throughout and be sure to land softly. Continue for the desired number of repetitions.

11 Butterfly crunch

Lying on your back, place your hands behind your ears to support your head. Bend your legs and drop your knees to the sides, placing the soles of your feet together. Maintaining a small gap between chin and chest, draw in your tummy muscles and exhale as you curl your shoulders off the ground. Inhale as you lower your shoulders to the ground to return to the start position. Continue for the desired number of repetitions.

Dumbbell arm extension 12

Hold a single weight between both hands and raise it above your head. Step one leg forwards and keep your tummy muscles drawn in. Inhale as you bend your elbows no more than to a right angle to lower the weight behind your head. Exhale as you semi-extend your arms to the start position. Continue for the desired number of repetitions.

Jogging heel up 13

Jog gently on the spot holding your hands behind your buttocks with your palms facing upwards. As you jog, gently kick your heels up towards your buttocks so your heels touch your palms. Keep your breathing regular throughout and be sure to land softly. Continue for the desired number of repetitions.

QUICK FIX PROGRAMME: Your day's been disrupted and you haven't exercised. Five minutes is all you need to choose five of your aerobic exercises and do 15 reps of each.

Regular

TONING PROGRAMME

Without good body tone there'll be little evidence of your sleek new look. These key toning exercises have been devised to allow you to specifically train for improvement in defining your muscles. Give two or three sets of 18–22 reps a try. Don't forget to pay particular attention to good technique and control.

1

Lying single arm extension

Works rear upper arms

Lying on your side, place your lower hand behind your head for support. Place your other arm across your chest, with your hand flat on the ground. Keeping your legs together, exhale as you semi-extend this arm to push your torso off the ground. Inhale as you lower your body to the ground to return to the start position. Continue for the desired number of repetitions then repeat on the other side.

2

All fours opposite arm and leg extension

Works lower back

Kneel on all fours, look straight ahead and keep your tummy muscles drawn in throughout. Simultaneously extend your left arm and raise your right leg. Hold for 5 seconds. Return to the start position, then repeat, alternating the arm and leg. Keep your breathing regular throughout. Continue for the desired number of repetitions.

3 Static crunch

Works abdominals

Lying on your back, raise both legs 45 degrees. Bend your right leg and stretch forwards with your left arm, placing your right hand behind your ear for support. With a small gap between chin and chest, exhale as you raise your head and shoulders and slide your left hand up your thigh. Hold for 5 seconds. Inhale as you briefly return to the start position. Continue for the desired number of repetitions, then change sides.

4 Static squat

Works thighs and buttocks

Stand with your back flat against a firm surface and your feet about a hip-width apart. Inhale as you bend your knees until your body forms a right angle. Keep your breathing regular throughout. Hold this position for a minimum of 30 seconds, then repeat. Continue for the desired number of repetitions.

5

Arm dip with elevated legs

Works rear upper arms, shoulders and chest

Sit on a firm seat, hands behind you, fingers facing forwards. Place your heels on a table or other support. Keeping your tummy muscles drawn in and your back straight, inhale as you bend your arms to a right angle and slowly lower your hips. Exhale as you semi-extend your arms to return. Continue for the desired number of repetitions.

6

Sideways single leg squat

Works upper thighs, buttocks and inner thighs

Stand sideways next to a support, placing the instep of the foot nearest to it on top. With your hands on your hips and a straight back, look straight ahead and inhale as you bend your supporting leg to no lower than a right angle. Exhale as you semi-extend your leg to return. Continue for the desired number of repetitions.

Remember to cool down and stretch (see pages 56–63).

1

2

14

13

Vigorous
AEROBIC CIRCUIT

12

11

10

This Vigorous programme is tougher, so you need to be ready to commit yourself to a routine that ties you down to training more frequently – four or five times each week. And if you've got this far, you may be ready to consider trying taking up a sport or other form of exercise. Choose something that interests you and complements your Triple A programme.

VIGOROUS AEROBIC CIRCUIT

Full press up

Lie face down with your feet slightly less than a hip-width apart and your hands at chest level, facing forwards. Semi-extend your arms to raise your body, steadying your weight equally over your arms and legs. Keeping your head up slightly, your tummy muscles drawn in and your legs straight, inhale as you bend your elbows to lower your chest almost to the ground. To return, semi-extend your arms as you exhale. Continue for the desired number of repetitions.

Star jump 2

Squat down slightly with your feet a hip-width apart and your hands in front of you. Exhale as you jump up into the air keeping your feet the same width apart. Simultaneously, raise your arms to form a star shape with your entire body. Inhale as you land softly, returning to the start position. Continue for the desired number of repetitions.

Sprint on the spot 3

Start running on the spot, raising your knees up to hip level and 'pumping' with your arms as if you were sprinting to catch the bus. Keep your breathing regular throughout. Continue for the desired length of time.

VIGOROUS AEROBIC CIRCUIT

4 Abdominal finger tap

Lying on your back, bend your knees and extend your arms along the sides of your body. Maintaining a small gap between chin and chest, exhale as you lift your shoulders off the ground and reach behind your thighs until your hands touch. To return, inhale as you lower your upper body. Continue for the desired number of repetitions.

5 Tuck jump

Stand with your feet slightly apart and your elbows partially bent. Exhale as you jump in the air, tucking your knees up and in towards your chest. Inhale as you land softly and in a well-controlled manner on the balls of your feet. Continue for the desired number of repetitions.

Shoulder 'V' press up

Kneel on all fours, with your hands wider than a shoulder-width apart and facing forwards. Extend your arms and straighten your legs to raise your body, steadying your weight equally over your arms and legs.

Inhale and keep your tummy muscles drawn in as you raise your buttocks upwards and bend your elbows to take your head and shoulders towards the ground. Your body will form a 'V' shape. Exhale as you extend your arms and lower your buttocks to return. Continue for the desired numberof repetitions.

6

VIGOROUS AEROBIC CIRCUIT

7 Shadow boxing

Start by jogging lightly on the spot, with arms bent, elbows tucked in and hands at chest level making a fist. Then punch out lightly with your left arm and return it, then repeat with the right arm, ensuring that you don't lock your elbows with each punch. Try a combination of punches, for example left, right, left, left, right, and so forth. Also try varying the power you use to punch. Keep your breathing regular throughout. Continue for the desired amount of time.

8 Elevated long crunch

Lying on your back, raise your legs until they are almost vertical. Extend your arms above your head, placing one hand over the other. 'Cup' your head between your upper arms for support. Now exhale as you raise your upper body off the ground and reach for your toes with both hands. Inhale as you lower yourself to return. Continue for the desired number of repetitions.

Running squat

Kneel on all fours, with your hands wider than a shoulder-width apart and facing forwards. Extend your arms and straighten your legs to raise your body, steadying your weight equally over your arms and legs. Keeping your tummy muscles drawn in, jump one leg in towards your hands, then jump it out again. Repeat using the other leg. Keep your breathing regular throughout. Continue for the desired number of repetitions.

Power leap

Stand with your knees partially bent, feet slightly apart and arms at your sides. Exhale as you leap upwards, bringing your arms up above your head. Inhale as you land softly and in a well-controlled manner bringing both feet flat on the ground again. Continue for the desired number of repetitions.

VIGOROUS AEROBIC CIRCUIT

11 Full press up with leg elevated

Lie face down, hands facing forwards at chest level and less than shoulder-width apart. Semi-extend your arms to raise yourself, steadying your weight equally over arms and legs. With head slightly up, tummy muscles in and legs straight, inhale as you bend your elbows to lower your chest almost to the ground, simultaneously raising one leg. Exhale as you semi-extend your arms to return. Repeat using the other leg. Continue for the desired number of repetitions.

12 Double knee to chest crunch

Lying on your back, support your head with your hands behind your ears. Raise both legs to a near vertical position. Exhale as you curl your upper body off the ground, bringing your knees towards your chest. Inhale as you lower your upper body to the ground to return. Continue for the desired number of repetitions.

Side leg kick

Stand with arms bent, elbows tucked in and hands at chest level making a fist. Exhale as you kick one leg out sideways, raising the elbow of the corresponding arm as you kick. Inhale as you return the leg and arm to the start position. Continue for the desired number of repetitions, then change legs.

Squat thrust

Kneel on all fours, with your hands wider than a shoulder-width apart and facing forwards. Extend your arms and straighten your legs to raise your body, steadying your weight equally over your arms and legs. Keeping your tummy muscles drawn in, inhale as you jump both legs together towards your hands, then exhale as you jump out again. Continue for the desired number of repetitions.

QUICK FIX PROGRAMME: Take a rejuvenating break from your hectic day by selecting six of your favourite aerobic exercises. Do a couple of sets of 15–20 reps to recharge your body.

Vigorous

TONING PROGRAMME

With this comprehensive super-sculpting programme, your body will be as taut and sleek as a shark's. Good technique, form and control are essential to build true muscle condition, so focus on these. You're in top shape, so aim high. Do at least three sets of 20–25 reps of each exercise to ensure maximum benefit.

1

Clapping full press up

Works upper body

Lie face down, hands at chest level and feet facing forwards. Extend arms fully to raise your body, weight equal over arms and legs. With head slightly up, tummy in and legs straight, inhale as you bend your elbows to lower your chest almost to the ground. Exhale as you return, pushing slightly off the ground and clapping with both hands. Inhale as you land on both hands. Continue for the desired number of repetitions.

2

Single leg extended arm dip

Works rear upper arms, shoulders and chest

Sit with hands behind you and palms facing forwards, slightly turned out. Bend one leg, resting the heel on the ground. Extend and raise the other leg. Lift your hips, keep your tummy muscles in and inhale as you bend the elbows to lower your buttocks. Exhale as you extend the arms to return. Avoid 'locking out' the elbows and thrusting the hips. Continue for the desired number of repetitions.

3
Oblique crunch
Works sides of waist

Lying on one side, place your lower arm across your ribcage and the other behind your head for support. Moving from your waist, exhale as you lift your upper body and arm, at the same time raising the corresponding knee to meet the elbow. Inhale as you lower to return. Continue for the desired number of repetitions, then change sides.

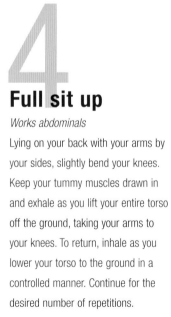

4
Full sit up
Works abdominals

Lying on your back with your arms by your sides, slightly bend your knees. Keep your tummy muscles drawn in and exhale as you lift your entire torso off the ground, taking your arms to your knees. To return, inhale as you lower your torso to the ground in a controlled manner. Continue for the desired number of repetitions.

5 Opposite arm and leg back extension

Works lower back

Lying on your front with your head down, raise and extend your right arm and left leg simultaneously. Hold for 5 seconds. Return to the start position, then repeat using left arm and right leg. Keep your breathing regular throughout. Continue, alternating sides, for the desired number of repetitions.

6 Hands under chin back extension

Works lower back

Lying on your front with your head down, place your hands under your chin, palms facing the ground. Slowly raise your head, shoulders and arms off the ground no more than 15–20cm. Hold for 5 seconds. Return to the start position for a second or two before repeating. Keep your breathing regular throughout. Continue for the desired number of repetitions.

Remember to cool down and stretch (see pages 56–63).

keep up the
GOOD WORK

Here I help you maintain your enthusiasm whatever stage of the Triple A programme you're at. If you've given up along the way, then maybe you just need to give your motivation a 'jump-start'. Re-evaluate where you are, follow my motivational tips and fill in your personal progress chart to help you log your journey to fitness. If you're nervous of exercising, my FAQs and facts about some of the great exercise myths should give you the confidence you need to get you going. And finally, if you've stuck to your programme, you'll have seen the huge benefits it brings. Hopefully your Triple A routine has now become a natural part of your lifestyle.

Keeping it going

Now you are pushing towards your health and fitness goals, you'll need to keep on top of your Triple A programme throughout the coming weeks and months. Most of you will be highly motivated during the early days and you should find working out using this plan exciting. But as time passes, it's easy to gradually slip back into unhealthy habits or to find an assortment of excuses for not exercising. To keep the fires of motivation burning, you must periodically supply some fuel. My motivational tips are just the fuel you need to make the flame burn brighter. These tips will help you add variety, provide you with new information and will give you reminders – all of which will help you keep up the enthusiasm and the desire to make these positive changes to your life. Just dip into this list from time to time – whenever you feel you might give up.

1 CREATE MENTAL IMAGES
Try to visualise how awful it would be to strip down to your beachwear on holiday only to be jeered at, or how bad you would feel if you couldn't get into the outfit you've bought for that special occasion. Then draw an imaginary large red line through these negative images and replace them with positive images of a slimmed-down, toned and energetic version of you – the benefits of sticking to your Triple A programme. You could also try getting hold of some visualisation tapes and play them each night before you go to bed. They really do work – and you'll find you get a better night's sleep too.

2 REMEMBER THAT FALLING BY THE WAYSIDE IS ONLY HUMAN
Maybe your old habits have crept back up on you or perhaps circumstances beyond your control have meant you couldn't manage to exercise one week. Don't let it get to you. Just get back on track as soon as you can and don't waste time punishing yourself.

3 SCARE YOURSELF INTO EXERCISE
This may sound drastic, but think what would happen if you don't change your bad habits but remain a sedentary blob. Think of the health costs of not exercising and how awful you would feel.

4 CHANGING YOUR NEGATIVE THOUGHTS
Recognise the negative thoughts that usually stop you from exercising, for example when you get home from work and tell yourself you're too tired to exercise. When you notice that a thought like this has come into your head, say 'Stop' to yourself and replace that thought with a positive one – such as 'I'm really tired, but I know that if I just make the effort to do my exercises, I'll feel better straight away'. It helps to have a list of positive thoughts already in your mind for when moments like this occur.

5 USE TANGIBLE MOTIVATORS SUCH AS PICTURES, POSTERS OR NOTES

If your aim is to lose weight, put up posters of people in great shape. Read magazines with real-life success stories of how people have managed to overcome their physical problems. These will offer you inspiration. Mark your calendar with dates for reaching your short-term goals and keep the calendar handy where you can easily see it.

6 KEEP TRACK OF YOUR PROGRESS

You'll feel more encouraged and motivated if you periodically check your progress against your initial goals every 2 or 3 months. For example, you may have found performing 15 press-ups a challenge at the start of your programme, so you decided then that doing 15 comfortably was to be your main aim over the following weeks. Look back and see how you've successfully achieved that aim. Doing 15 press-ups is now a piece of cake! Once you've reached a goal, set a new one so that you're constantly aiming to do better.

7 PUMP UP YOUR MOTIVATION BY AIMING FOR THE NEXT LEVEL IN THE TRIPLE A PROGRAMME

For example, if you're an Exercise Restarter, relish the idea of moving forwards to becoming a Regular Exerciser.

8 CHANGE YOUR WORKOUT VENUE

The Triple A system is designed to be done anywhere. Occasionally, being or doing things in the same place for too long can result in tedium. If you usually perform your workout indoors, try moving to your garden or local park for a refreshing new environment. After all, a change is as good as a rest.

9 LISTENING TO MUSIC OR HAVING THE TELEVISION ON IN THE BACKGROUND WHILE YOU DO YOUR TRIPLE A WORKOUT CAN MAKE A PLEASANT DISTRACTION

Ideally, listening to faster music with a good tempo and rhythm to match your exercise pace is best for the aerobic section of your workout, while slower, calmer music would be more suited to the cool-down and stretching phases.

10 BE OPTIMISTIC BUT REALISTIC

Make yourself aware that changes take time and that you will experience occasional setbacks. If you find you are not getting the results you want, be patient and stick with it. If you work at something hard enough, changes have to occur. If you miss a workout or sometimes go off the rails with your eating, forgive yourself and continue with your programme. We are all human and these 'hiccups' are quite natural.

11 GET GOOD SUPPORT

Tell your friends about your fitness campaign. Ask them for their help and encouragement. Get them to support you if you feel as if you're falling by the wayside. Teach them to identify what distracts you from exercising, so they can help you get back on track whenever necessary.

12 FINALLY, RESORT TO SELF–BLACKMAIL

Every time you skip a workout, stuff yourself silly with chocolate pudding or indulge in a boozing binge, donate at least £10 of your hard-earned cash to your favourite charity.

If you follow all of my suggestions in this section for maintaining motivation, you are bound to succeed eventually. Keep with it – it's worth it!

Personal progress chart

Charting your progress helps you stick to a programme consistently and remain motivated. I've designed this user-friendly chart to make record-keeping as easy as possible. After all, I'm sure you'd rather spend your valuable time doing your Triple A workout than sitting and writing about it! The first column gives an example of how someone might have filled in the chart after their first week. Now it's up to you. Be honest with yourself and fill the chart in each week. Good luck.

NUMBER OF WORKOUTS FOR THE WEEK	EXAMPLE	WEEK 1	WEEK 2	WEEK 3	WEEK 4	WEEK 5	WEEK 6
Exercise Newcomer Exercise Restarter Regular Exerciser Vigorous Exerciser	2						
HOW YOU FELT DURING THE WEEK							
Exhausted Fairly tired Irritable/Moody Bored Relaxed Fine Energised In control	Yes						
HOW YOU FELT BEFORE YOUR EXERCISE SESSION							
Tired Reluctant Lacking motivation Raring to go	Yes						
HOW YOU FELT DURING YOUR EXERCISE SESSION							
All exercises were tough Some exercises were hard	Yes						

HOW YOU FELT DURING YOUR EXERCISE SESSION	EXAMPLE	WEEK 1	WEEK 2	WEEK 3	WEEK 4	WEEK 5	WEEK 6
Comfortable The exercises were easy I could do more	Yes						
HOW YOU FELT AFTER YOUR EXERCISE SESSION							
Invigorated							
Fine	Yes						
Tired							
Exhausted	No						
INDICATE YOUR EATING HABITS							
Controlled	Yes						
Well planned							
Hopeless							
Binged							
Increased fruit intake	Yes						
Decreased fruit intake							
Increased vegetable intake							
Decreased vegetable intake	Yes						
Increased water intake	Yes						
Decreased water intake							
Increased fat intake							
Decreased fat intake	Yes						
Eaten take-aways	Twice						
Excess sugar intake	Yes						
Lowered sugar intake							
Excess dairy products							
Lowered dairy products	Yes						
HOW YOU FEEL ABOUT WHAT YOU'VE MANAGED TO ACHIEVE DURING THE WEEK							
Failed miserably							
Achieved very little							
Achieved most of my goals	Yes						
Achieved all of my goals and more							

Cornel's Frequently Asked Questions

Whether you have already started trying out one of my Triple A exercise programmes, or are thinking of doing so, I'm sure there are a lot of unanswered questions buzzing around in your head. Here I have made a selection of some of the most popular and frequently asked exercise queries that have been put to me over the years that I've been a personal trainer.

Q I am pregnant and wish to continue exercising during my pregnancy. Is it safe to do so?

A Expectant mothers can safely exercise right up to the latter stages of pregnancy, though it is important first to understand that pregnancy is a time of change that puts added demands on the expectant mother's entire system. These changes can be handled in many positive ways, possibly the best way being exercise. However, you should bear in mind that pregnancy is a time to maintain fitness and prepare for labour, not a time to try and significantly improve your fitness levels. Pregnancy also offers the opportunity to follow an exercise programme that will help develop a healthy lifestyle – one that you can continue after the birth. If you are pregnant it is advisable to seek the advice of your doctor or exercise professional before you start any exercise programme.

Q I am now 65 years of age and retired. I wish to spend a lot of my spare time looking after myself and exercising is at the top of my 'must do' list. Can a person of my age expect any real results from exercising?

A During the first 30 years of our lives, strength and muscle mass increase steadily as we grow but after the age of 30 we lose about 1 per cent per year of muscular strength, mass and cardiovascular fitness. However, our lifestyle has a direct effect on these ageing processes and research shows that we can preserve all of the above, no matter at what age we begin and maintain a regular exercise programme. So it's never too late!

Q I experience occasional fatigue and find it difficult to exercise. What can I do to overcome this?

A Nearly all of us experience fatigue at some time, and many of us have consulted a doctor about it. Fatigue can be brought on by several factors – for instance, lack of sleep, poor diet, stress, depression or periods of inactivity. It may also be a symptom of serious illness, such as anaemia, diabetes, chronic fatigue syndrome, lung disease, heart disease, thyroid problems and cancer.

If you are generally healthy, then the key to fighting fatigue is to eat properly and take up exercise. If you're a smoker, you should try giving up. You'll also benefit greatly from keeping an eye on your weight, examining your diet, and reducing your stress levels and alcohol intake.

Q I have been diagnosed with osteoporosis. My doctor has advised me to take up regular exercise and to change my eating habits. Can the Triple A exercise system be of any benefit to me?

A Osteoporosis – more common in postmenopausal women and those over 50 years of age – is the most common disorder of the skeleton. Cigarette smokers, alcohol users, those who are sedentary and fervent dieters are also at risk. It is a disease in which there is a decrease in the amount of bone mass. This deficiency creates weak and frail bones, which leads to numerous problems. One of the most effective ways to combat osteoporosis is to exercise. The Triple A Exercise Newcomer programme would be ideal for you. I also recommend a proper eating plan offering adequate levels of calcium, vitamins and other minerals, and no fewer than 1,200 calories for women and 1,500 calories for men.

Q I have read that research demonstrates that exercise is a more effective way of relieving depression than the use of medication. Since I suffer from depression, what can I expect from exercise?

A Depression is widespread and can be debilitating and potentially life-threatening, lasting for months or even years. It is characterised as a mental condition of gloom, sadness or dejection. Possibly the most effective way to reduce depression is through aerobic exercise. This has been shown to bring about a significant reduction in anxiety and depression, since increasing evidence shows that exercise stimulates the body's production of endorphins – the body's natural pain killers that also contribute to feelings of overall wellbeing. Working with your Triple A plan is an excellent way to enjoy the benefits of aerobic exercise.

Q I suffer from diabetes and wish to exercise. What considerations apply when exercising for someone with my disorder?

A There are two forms of diabetes. Type I – Insulin-Dependent Diabetes Mellitus (IDDM) is associated with a deficiency of insulin production. Type II – Non-Insulin Dependent Diabetes Mellitus (NIDDM), or mature-onset diabetes, is associated with decreased insulin sensitivity or obesity. Around 93 per cent of all diabetics have NIDDM and 85 per cent of these are obese at their time of diagnosis.

Treatment centres around the control of blood glucose levels, achieved through insulin, diet and exercise. Regular aerobic exercise will decrease insulin requirements by 30–50 per cent in people with well-controlled IDDM and by 100 per cent in those with NIDDM. It is estimated that with diet and exercise, only 25 per cent of diabetics would need medication.

If you are diabetic you need to take certain precautions when exercising:

- Monitor your blood glucose levels prior to exercise.
- Type I diabetics may decrease their insulin dose or increase their carbohydrate intake prior to exercise as recommended by a doctor.
- Type I diabetics should avoid injecting insulin into muscle areas that will be active during exercise.
- Type I diabetics should avoid exercise during times when insulin reaches peak effectiveness.
- Short-acting carbohydrates should be available for hypoglycaemia reactions.
- Carbohydrates may be eaten during prolonged exercise sessions.
- Exercise one hour after meals, when blood glucose is at its peak.
- You should only exercise after checking with your doctor.

Q Can I become addicted to exercise?

A After exercise many people report less stress, irritation, depression and anxiety. They also enjoy improved self-esteem and the ability to concentrate both during and for several hours following exercise. Some exercisers experience feelings of euphoria, serenity and of being one with the activity.

People who enjoy exercise are most likely to exercise often and they may feel a bit depressed if anything prevents them from doing so. This sort of dedication to exercise is not unhealthy. Symptoms of unhealthy exercise addiction would include exercising during injury or against medical advice, or feeling that exercise is more important than anything else in life, including work and family. If you feel that you may fall into this category, it's time to rethink your exercise programme. What's important is to do the amount and type of exercise that's appropriate for you. Trying to overdo it will more than likely lead to frustration and injury rather than euphoria. Make sure your programme includes the activities you enjoy most. Chart your progress and remind yourself of your health and fitness goals.

Q I suffer from high blood pressure. What tips can you offer me to help control this condition and is it safe to take up exercise?

EXPLODING THE GREAT EXERCISE MYTHS

Every day the media bombards us with information on exercise, health and diets. No wonder it can be difficult for the would-be-exerciser to sort the fact from the fiction. Triple A helps you make up your mind about some of the most popular misconceptions, but in case you're still unsure, here are some more home truths.

1 MYTH Regularly doing sit-up exercises will give me a six-pack, washboard stomach.

FACT You can do all the sit-ups in the world but they won't give you a flat, fat-free stomach. Regularly combining sit-ups for tone and doing some form of aerobic exercise to burn off fat is the key to that desirable six-pack. And by the way, stuffing yourself with chocolates and cream cakes won't help either, so it's wise to eat healthily too.

2 MYTH Unfit people sweat more that fit people.
FACT Sweating is the way your body responds when you get hot. In fact, fit individuals sweat more when exercising than the not-so-fit since exercise makes the body more efficient at cooling down.

3 MYTH Women who lift weights will build up big, bulky and unsightly muscles.

FACT Incorporating a comprehensive weight training programme into your exercise regime won't bulk you up if you are a woman, as women do not possess high levels of testosterone – the muscle-developing male hormone. Instead, weight training will firm and tone your muscles and will improve your overall posture. Everyone can benefit from the improved muscle condition to be obtained from lifting weights. It will also increase your metabolism and so encourage your body to burn more calories. Ultimately this leads to improved weight management.

4 MYTH Myth: Skinny people are healthier and fitter.
FACT Health and fitness are not just to do with weight. Slim people are susceptible to poor muscle tone, lack of cardiovascular fitness and high levels of body fat, while thin people can be more prone to osteoporosis (see page 123). They all need to exercise just like everyone else.

Today, high blood pressure is one of the main causes of death. More than half the people suffering from high blood pressure are unaware of it. Blood pressure is the measure of the force that the heart needs to pump the blood through the circulatory system. The higher the pressure, the harder the heart has to work. Blood pressure is measured in 2 parts:

Systolic This results from the heart's contraction as blood is ejected from the ventricles into the body, and is indicated by the first, or top, number of the blood-pressure reading.

Diastolic This phase results from the relaxation of the heart as blood fills its chambers, and is indicated by the second, or lower, number of the blood-pressure reading. A normal blood-pressure reading is about 120/80.

To combat high blood pressure :

- Have your blood pressure checked regularly.
- Control your weight.
- Take medication if prescribed by your doctor.
- Relax daily and try to limit amount of stress in your life.
- Reduce your salt intake.
- Do some exercise. Regular exercise is proven to decrease your blood pressure by strengthening your cardiovascular system and helping the heart to become more efficient. Consult your doctor or exercise professional first.

5 MYTH I can get into great shape just by running.
FACT Although running has many merits, unfortunately you can't get away with it that easily! Just like running, swimming, dancing and cycling will go a long way towards improving your general stamina, but they cannot be considered to be the 'complete' workout. As well as building stamina, you need a workout that includes stretching to improve flexibility and weight training for muscle tone and bone strengthening. In other words, you should try to cross train – incorporating a variety of activities to give a more balanced approach to your workout schedule. This is what the Triple A system is all about!

6 MYTH No pain, no gain!
FACT Exercising is not the easiest thing in the world. When you do exercise your body will be going through some amazing changes and it is quite normal to experience some slight discomfort from time to time. However, exercise shouldn't hurt. Pain is your body telling you that something is wrong and that you should stop. Going beyond the pain barrier can lead to untold injury

7 MYTH When you stop exercising your muscles turn to fat.
FACT This is absolutely untrue and a physiological impossibility. Discontinuing aerobic exercise and continuing to eat the same amount of calories as when you were exercising will lead to muscle shrinkage and an increase in fat levels. This gives a smoother appearance to the body, but is as a result of the lost muscle tone.

8 MYTH Exercising every day will be better for me.
FACT Intense, heavy exercise on a daily basis will not only make you feel tired, but can even hinder your progress. Your body needs time to recover and repair itself after a hard workout. Gentle activities such walking, light swimming or biking are fine to do each day, but it is best to limit your more intense workouts, such as weight training or heavy aerobic exercise, to every other day.

Index

ACKNOWLEDGEMENTS

Acknowledgements

I dedicate this book to my uncle Kenneth 'Rex' Chin (8 February 1935–20 January 2002), who throughout my youth set me on the pathway to realising the benefits of a healthier lifestyle.

This book was born as a collective result of inspiration and encouragement from my family and friends. I wish to acknowledge the support, enthusiasm and commitment shown by them, particularly to my wife, Ania Ansikiewicz-Chin, my brothers Ian and Darren Chin and to mum and dad, for their unconditional love and wisdom.

I am most grateful to my literary agent, Elizabeth Puttick, for her devotion, time and effort and for steering me in the right direction in the vast world of publishing.

A mammoth thank you is in order to two of my best friends David Arden and Andrew Prockter for their support, copy reading and especially for helping me when my computer didn't do what I wanted it to do.

A big thank you to my close friends, for their time and sweat, and for patiently posing for the photographs in this book: my wife Ania (model for the Newcomer), Errol Arthur (model for the Vigorous), Adrian 'But ahm' Bowden (model for the Restarter) and Lorraine Forest (model for the Regular).

An extra special thank you must go to Hilary Mandleberg, for her expertise and steadfast dedication at every stage of this book as the project editor.

Thanks to the talented Leonardo DiCaprio, Colin Firth and Audrey Tautou for their support and testimonials for this book.

Thanks and praise to the team at Quadrille Publishing Ltd, especially to Amanda Lerwill, for creating the book's beautiful 'look' and to Graham Atkin Hughes, for his photographic expertise.

Thank you to Blueridge.co.uk, who provided the beautiful workout wear for the models.

Many thanks to Nick Tsavalos for his support and martial arts expertise.

Finally, I would like to add a very special thanks to all of my clients for their understanding, support and for 'giving me time off' to write this book: Toni & Jerrold Assersohn; Brian Barclay; Jane Barclay; John Battsek; Deborah Battsek; Roy Bensusan; Janine Roxborough-Bunce; Reg Burr; Rosemary Burr; Raquel Cassidy; Jo Craig; Anthony Doran; Rachael Fleming; David Gill; Henni and Irving Goldstein; Gerard Ayrton-Grime; Gilda Hamilton; Meg Jansz; Andrew Macdonald; Mary Madigan; Peter Magyar; Barbara Maher; Anne-Katrin Meier; Juliette Owide; Paula Shaw; Doris Sherwood; Siobhan Squire; Labis and Sophie Tsirigotakis; Lynn Vanvarik; Danielle Webb and Natascha Wharton.

For more fitness advice and information, Cornel's website can be visited at: www.cmcfit.co.uk